SCALE YOUR INCOME

In loving memory of Dan Miller,

Your guidance and teachings on the art of decision-making (48 days or less) and creating multiple streams of income left an indelible mark on my life and work. You inspired me to live with purpose and share that message with the world.

Your legacy will continue to impact countless lives through the wisdom you imparted.

SCALE YOUR INCOME

The 48-day income blueprint to create
multiple streams of revenue as a writer,
coach, teacher, or speaker

Jonathan Milligan

PGB

PLATFORM GROWTH BOOKS

Book Cover by Platform Growth Books

Illustrations by Jonathan Milligan

1st edition 2024

YOUR FREE GIFT

As a way of saying thanks for your purchase, we are offering a free companion online course called, ***The Scale Your Income Accelerator Course.***

With this companion online course, you'll be able to fully implement all the exercises, worksheets, and checklists inside this book. To get free instant access, go to:

MarketYourMessage.com/scale-course

	Mini	Main	Max
Writer	Low-Content Book	Compact Book	Book Series
Teacher	Mini-Course	Flagship Course	Membership Site
Speaker	Paid Virtual Workshop	Paid Speaking Gigs	Host In-Person Events
Coach	4-Week Group Coaching	1-on-1 Coaching	Coaching Membership

The Messenger Product Map

Inside the pages of this book, you'll discover the Messenger Product Map. To scale your income, you need to amplify your message into multiple income streams: Writer (books), Teacher (courses), Speaker (events), and Coach (programs).

Contents

Introduction

S tart before you are ready.

Have you ever felt like you're constantly learning but not seeing the results you hoped for? You've read the books, taken the courses, and maybe even attended a few workshops, but nothing seems to stick. That's because there's a gap between learning and action—a gap where most people get stuck.

So, why do some people make massive strides while others stay in place?

It's not a lack of knowledge. It's something more profound. The reality is that the more you wait, the harder it gets to take action. We tell ourselves we need more time, information, or confidence. But that's just the trap—the readiness mirage. The truth is clarity doesn't come before action. It comes *through* action.

I know this feeling all too well. I spent years in the "learning zone," always preparing for the "perfect time" to launch my ideas. I convinced myself that more planning was the key to success. Yet, the more I planned, the less I moved forward. Fear and doubt kept me frozen. What if I failed? What if no one cared about my message? What if I wasn't good enough?

But what if there's another way? What if you took imperfect action instead of waiting until everything was perfect? What if you could quickly validate your ideas, turn your knowledge into income streams, and scale them into a thriving business without burning out?

That's what this book is about.

For over a decade, I've helped writers, coaches, speakers, and course creators. I've shown them how to transform their message into multiple income streams. The process I'll show you isn't just theory. It's a proven approach that thousands of people like you have used to build businesses they love while reclaiming their time and freedom.

Imagine having a business that runs smoothly while you're off doing things you love. Imagine creating meaningful products that serve your audience without constantly trading hours for dollars. Imagine waking up to new sales notifications from offers you've already created. It's not a dream; it's a system.

That system is what you'll learn in this book.

I'll teach you to scale your income using the Messenger Product Map. It's a framework for turning your message into multiple income streams. This is how you leverage your expertise into books, courses, coaching programs, and more—without feeling overwhelmed or stuck in the "one-trick pony" trap.

Here's what you can expect from this book:

- You'll discover how to create low-content products quickly to validate your ideas.

- I'll walk you through how to expand those ideas into deeper, more valuable offers.

- You'll discover how to stack your income streams to free up your time while growing your revenue.

This book is for you whether you're just starting or looking to scale your existing business. It's for the person who's ready to take action and wants to create a business that survives and thrives.

Now is the time to stop learning and start doing. By the time you finish this book, you'll have the tools and confidence to take that next step, and the one after that, until you've built something you're proud of.

Let's get started. The life you've been working for is within reach.

1

The Multiple Income Streams of a Messenger

T oys 'R' Us was a household name. You couldn't think of toys without picturing those huge stores filled with endless aisles of games, action figures, and bikes. They had it all. But when e-commerce started taking over, they stuck to what they knew best—physical stores. They even handed over their online sales to Amazon. Why build their own platform when they could just ride Amazon's coattails?

But as more and more people shopped online, Toys 'R' Us couldn't keep up. Amazon, Walmart, and other e-commerce giants took over the toy market, and eventually, the company filed for bankruptcy in 2017[1]. The lesson is clear: when you rely on one thing, you're vulnerable to a changing world.

You see this happen all the time in the influencer and content creator world. People fall into the one-trick pony trap. They focus on just one income stream, hoping it'll be their big break. For some, it's churning out book after book. For others, it's coaching one client at a time, grinding out hour after hour. It's easy to get stuck in this cycle.

But here's the thing—it's a recipe for frustration. When you pour all your energy into just one thing, you put all your eggs in one basket. And if something changes? You're left scrambling.

Why It's a Recipe for Frustration

- **Limited Reach:** You're only talking to one type of audience. Not everyone wants to read books or sit in on a coaching call. People learn differently, and sticking to one format leaves a huge chunk of potential followers out.

- **Vulnerability:** What happens if your chosen platform suddenly changes its rules? Maybe the algorithm shifts, or your clients dry up. When all your income depends on one stream, you're at the mercy of forces beyond your control.

- **Missed Opportunities:** You've got a message. You've got ideas. But if you're focused on one thing, you leave money on the table. You could reach more people and make a bigger impact, but you're too busy trying to keep that one trick going.

The one-trick pony trap feels safe at first. But in the long run, it's risky. It's time to think bigger.

A Better Way: The Holistic Approach

The good news? There's a way out. It's about seeing your content as more than just a book or a course. It's a message that can live in a hundred different forms. Think about multiplying your message instead of relying on just one income stream. You could write books, create courses, offer coaching, speak at events—the options are endless. Imagine having multiple income streams all feeding into each other. You're no longer stuck on one thing. You're free to adapt, evolve, and grow.

Identify Your Influencer Voices

Ever feel like you're wearing just one hat, day in and day out? It's time to mix it up. You've got four main voices to choose from: writer, teacher, speaker, and coach. Each one is like a tool in your toolbox, waiting to be used.

Picture yourself as a bandleader. Maybe writing is your go-to instrument, like a steady drumbeat. But what if you could add a little flair with some coaching (the guitar riff)? Or go big with speaking (think of it like the trumpet solo). The more you try, the richer the performance. Find the one that feels natural, but don't stop there. Try on the others—you might surprise yourself with what fits.

Understand the Three Offer Types

Let's break down your income streams into three categories: Mini, Main, and Max offers. These aren't just buzzwords—they're your keys to scaling up. Don't think of them in terms of mini offers, which are the lowest-priced products, and max offers, which are higher priced. Pricing can vary throughout the Messenger Product Map. Instead I want you to view them as a difficulty scale. Mini offers are fast to create. Max offers take more work to launch, but the rewards make it worthwhile.

Let's break each type of offer down:

- **Mini offers are your quick wins.** They're simple, fast, and easy to sell. Think of them as appetizers for your business. They give people a taste without a big commitment.

- **Main offers are where you build stability.** These take more time and effort, but they're the bread and butter of your business.

- **Max offers are the game changers.** These require the most work but can bring in the big bucks. Think of them as your full-course meal—your most valuable offering.

Now, let's examine how these offers fit into the income streams of writers, teachers, speakers, and coaches.

The Writer Income Streams

Got that writing itch? Let's turn it into cash.

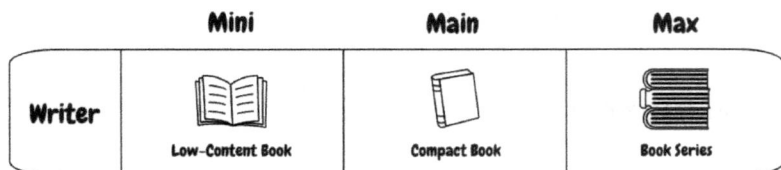

Writer	Mini	Main	Max
	Low-Content Book	Compact Book	Book Series

Start with low-content books—things like journals, planners, or workbooks. They're quick to create and great for testing the waters. You can knock these out in a week or two, like sprinting to the finish line.

Then, there are compact books. These are your mid-range projects. Aim for around 30,000 words. Think of them as your steady jog, pacing yourself for consistent earnings.

Finally, the book series. This is your marathon. It might take a while to build, but the long-term payoff can be huge. Think of your writing as a garden. Low-content books are your fast-growing veggies. Compact books are the sturdy perennials. Your book series is a fruit tree. It takes time to grow, but it keeps giving.

The Teacher Income Streams

Got knowledge? Let's turn that into a revenue stream. Are you a teacher at heart? If so, you can create three main types of income streams.

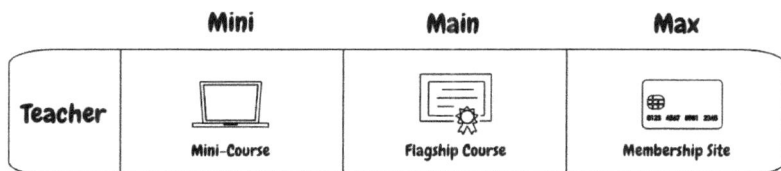

	Mini	Main	Max
Teacher	Mini-Course	Flagship Course	Membership Site

Mini-courses are a great way to start. They are short, sweet, and focused—think 8 to 12 videos on a specific topic. You could whip one of these up over a weekend.

Flagship courses go deeper. You're looking at 3-6 modules packed with content. This is where you really dive in.

Then there's the ultimate: a membership site. This takes more work upfront, but it's where the magic of recurring income happens. You create a community where students keep coming back month after month.

The Speaker Income Streams

It's time to let your voice be heard—and paid for. In this book, we will cover three types of speaker income streams.

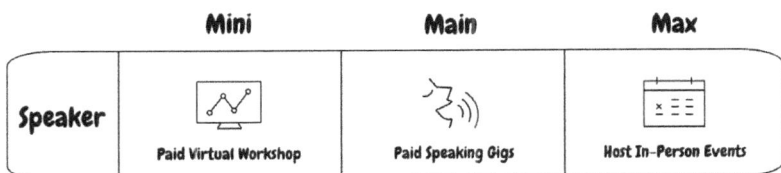

	Mini	Main	Max
Speaker	Paid Virtual Workshop	Paid Speaking Gigs	Host In-Person Events

Paid virtual workshops are a great starting point. Post an idea on social media, see who's interested, and deliver a workshop on Zoom.

Next, step it up to paid speaking gigs. You'll need a demo reel and some polished topics. Once you've got those, you're ready to pitch yourself for bigger events.

And then, there are in-person events. This is where the magic happens. Whether it's a small group paying $5,000 each or a larger crowd at $200 a head, live events can make a lasting impact.

Imagine throwing a pebble into a pond. Virtual workshops create little ripples. Paid gigs? Bigger waves. In-person events are the splash that reaches far beyond the initial impact.

The Coach Income Streams

Ready to start coaching? Let's map it out.

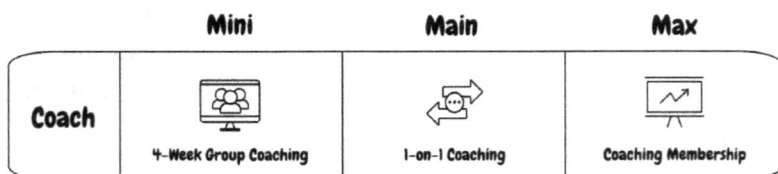

	Mini	Main	Max
Coach			
	4-Week Group Coaching	1-on-1 Coaching	Coaching Membership

A four-week group coaching program is your quick win. Sell it first, build it later, and get a feel for what your audience really wants.

One-on-one coaching is your mainstay. It's the bread and butter of personal development. Get that 'Work with Me' page up and decide how you want clients to book—talk first or pay first?

For the big leagues, go for high-ticket coaching memberships. Imagine coaching 50 people at once in just a couple of hours each week. It's a scalable way to offer massive value without burning out.

Maximize your clients' potential by giving them tools and guidance they can use to succeed on their own. Later in this book, we will show you exactly how to build each offer in your business.

Integrate and Optimize Your Income Streams

Now, the fun part—tying it all together.

Look at your income streams like pieces of a puzzle. How do they fit together? Maybe content from one feeds into another. For example, could a mini-course be an intro to your flagship course?

Balance is everything. You want a mix of quick wins, steady earners, and long-term investments. It's like managing an investment portfolio. Diversify to minimize risk and boost your returns, but make sure each part supports your overall goals.

Later in this book, we will dive deep into five different scaling blueprints you could use. The good news is you can run a profitable online business by implementing just one of the scaling blueprints.

Today's Exercise: Mapping Your Messenger Product Portfolio

It's time to map out your own Messenger Product Portfolio. This exercise is designed just to get your wheels turning. In the chapters ahead, you'll learn five different income scaling blueprints you could implement.

Start by listing all your current income streams. Be thorough. That ebook you wrote last year? Jot it down. Are there coaching calls you do twice a month? That counts, too.

Now, let's categorize. Which of these fall under Writer, Teacher, Speaker, or Coach? Draw four columns and sort your income streams accordingly. Don't worry if some columns are empty - that's valuable information.

Next, let's go deeper. For each income stream, decide if it's a Mini, Main, or Max offer. Remember, this isn't about price - it's about complexity and time investment. Mark each one accordingly.

Take a step back. What do you notice? Are you heavy in one area and light in others? That's your opportunity for growth.

Here's where it gets exciting. For each influencer type you're not currently using, brainstorm at least one new income stream. Let your imagination run wild. What Mini offer could you create as a Speaker? Is there a Max offer waiting to be born in your Teacher category?

Now, choose one. Just one new income stream that excites you. Got it? Great. Let's make it happen.

Outline the steps you'd need to create and launch this new stream within the next 48 days. Be specific. What resources do you need? Who could help you? What's your timeline?

Finally, reflect. How does this new stream complement your existing offers? How does it support your overall business goals? Write down your thoughts.

Congratulations! You've just taken the first step towards diversifying your income and scaling your impact. How does it feel to see your potential laid out in front of you?

Remember, this is a living document. Come back to it regularly, update it, and watch your Messenger Product Portfolio grow and evolve. What will you tackle first?

Key Takeaways:

- Diversifying your income across the four influencer types (Writer, Teacher, Speaker, Coach) can greatly boost your earnings and business stability.

- Balance Mini, Main, and Max offers to create a mix of quick wins, stable income, and long-term growth opportunities.

- A single message or area of expertise can be leveraged across multiple formats and income streams, maximizing its value and reach.

2

The Magic of 48 Days

I first heard Dan Miller on Dave Ramsey's radio show while driving to my evening job at a call center. I'd picked that job because it left my days open to start a business. But after several months, I hadn't taken a single step toward that goal. The daily grind had a way of swallowing up my ambitions. As I navigated the familiar route to work, the voice on the radio started talking about a book called *48 Days to the Work You Love*. The title grabbed me. It felt like a sign.

Stuck in traffic and stuck in life, I listened as Dan shared his message about moving forward before you feel ready. His words hit me like a jolt of electricity. Here was someone telling me that 48 days was all it took to make a significant change. Not years of planning, not waiting for the perfect moment—just a decisive period of action. It was both terrifying and exhilarating.

I'd been clinging to the idea that I needed more time, more resources, more everything before I could start my own business. Dan was challenging that notion head-on. He was saying that action comes first, and clarity follows. That you don't wait for confidence—you build it through doing. Sitting there in my car, I felt a spark ignite.

Dan became more than just a voice on the radio. He became a mentor and eventually a friend. His lessons reshaped how I approached my career and my life. He taught me two truths: start before you're ready. And, you can create multiple income streams from a single message. These weren't just ideas—they became the foundation of everything I do.

In this chapter, we'll explore these two transformative lessons. We'll dive into the concept of the 48-day timeline and how it can propel you into action. Then we'll look at how one core message can blossom into multiple avenues of income and impact. This isn't just about honoring Dan's legacy; it's about equipping you to create meaningful change in your own life.

The Waiting Game

Most people have a story they tell themselves about why they haven't started. They need more information. They're not quite ready yet. There's a little more research to do, a few more boxes to check, or a little more time to get everything in order. The truth is that the "someday" they're waiting for never comes. Life keeps moving, and the perfect moment they've been holding out for is just an illusion.

This leads to an endless loop of preparation. It's the easy way out, really. Planning feels productive, but it's a smokescreen for inaction. We convince ourselves we're making progress when, in reality, we're just spinning our wheels. Opportunities pass by, and we're left on the sidelines, wondering why we haven't moved forward. The more we plan, the less we actually *do*.

The Readiness Mirage

Here's the catch: No one ever truly feels "ready." Readiness is a moving target. The more you wait, the further it drifts. There's always something else to learn, something else to tweak. But the longer you hesitate, the bigger the leap feels. Waiting doesn't reduce the risk; it amplifies the fear.

The irony? Taking action—any action—immediately starts to build the confidence you thought you needed in the first place. Clarity doesn't come from more preparation; it comes from *doing*. The moment you start, things begin to make sense. You see what works and what doesn't. You course-correct. But that shift only happens once you're already in motion.

Just Take the First Step

Dan's core philosophy was simple: you don't need to have everything figured out to get started. Take the first step, even if it's small, even if it's messy. Start before you're ready, and figure it out as you go. Momentum builds quickly when you stop overthinking and start acting. The longer you sit on the sidelines, the harder it gets to take that leap.

The magic of the 48-day timeline is that it forces you to act. It gives you a window—not too long to overthink, but long enough to make real progress. You set a short, decisive deadline and go. The timeline pushes you out of the waiting zone and into the doing zone. Instead of endlessly preparing, you're executing, refining, and learning.

If you wait until you're ready, you'll wait forever. Instead, trust that the path will become clearer with every step you take. Progress happens when you start moving, not when you're standing still.

The Power of 48 Days: Start Before You Are Ready

Forty-eight days is a sweet spot. It's long enough to take real, measurable action but short enough to force you into motion. When we're given too much time, we tend to overthink, second-guess, and lose momentum. The magic of 48 days lies in its urgency. You don't have time to get bogged down in perfectionism or endless preparation. You're forced to act, to make decisions quickly, and to learn as you go.

When I first embraced the 48-day timeline, I was stuck—spinning my wheels, waiting for the right moment. Dan's message changed everything. Instead of waiting for clarity, I started moving, even though I didn't have all the answers. And that's when things started to shift. Taking small steps each day, I began to find direction. The act of *doing* cleared the fog that endless planning never could.

What if you gave yourself the same challenge? Commit to 48 days. Set a deadline for a specific goal and start moving. Don't worry about having all the pieces in place. Start with what you know and adjust along the way. Make decisions faster, take action daily, and watch as momentum builds. You'll discover that clarity isn't a prerequisite for action—it's a result of it.

Building Multiple Income Streams from One Message

Dan's story began in a simple Sunday school class, where he helped people navigate career transitions. He didn't set out to build an empire. He saw a need, filled it, and let the journey unfold. The key? He didn't wait for everything to be perfect—he started with what he had. Over time, that core message of helping people find meaningful work grew into something much bigger. He created a best-selling book, seminars, coaching programs, a membership site, and even a certification program. One message: many income streams.

Dan didn't reinvent the wheel with every new product. He took what he already knew and repurposed it in different formats to reach more people. The book became a workbook, an online seminar, and a coaching program. Each new income stream was an extension of his original message.

I've followed the same path in my business. What began as teaching others how to build an audience online evolved into books, courses, workshops, and memberships. Each one was rooted in the same core message but offered in a new format or context. This is how you build multiple income streams without burning out. It's not about creating entirely new ideas; it's about finding new ways to share the ideas you already have.

The lesson is simple: focus on one core message that resonates with your audience and find ways to offer it across multiple platforms. A book becomes a course. A course becomes a coaching program. A coaching program becomes a membership site. When you leverage your message in different ways, you're not just building a business—you're building a sustainable, thriving income.

Today's Exercise: The 48-Day Practice Run

Let's put this into action. Think of this exercise as a warm-up for what's to come. Later in the book, you'll dive into more specific strategies for creating multiple income streams. But for now, this is about getting you into motion. It's about building momentum by tackling a goal you've been putting off.

Here's how you can start:

- **Step 1: Pick Your Goal.** Choose one project, idea, or business goal you've been sitting on. It doesn't have to be perfect or fully fleshed out. It might be an idea for a book, a course, a product, or even a business you've thought about starting. Don't overthink it. The goal here is action, not perfection.

- **Step 2: Write It Down.** Put that goal on paper. It doesn't matter if it feels vague or uncertain right now. What matters is that you've identified it. Sometimes, just writing down the goal makes it feel more real.

- **Step 3: Set Your 48-Day Deadline.** Commit to making progress on that goal over the next 48 days. This isn't about completing the entire project—this is about taking concrete action and moving forward. Choose a date 48 days from today and circle it on your calendar.

- **Step 4: Break It Down.** Now, let's divide those 48 days into manageable chunks:

  - **First 6 Days**: Map out your plan. Ask yourself *why* this goal matters and *what* you hope to achieve. Don't get caught up in the "how" just yet—that will come later. Focus on your purpose and vision.

  - **Next 5 Weeks**: Begin executing the plan. Break your big goal into smaller, weekly tasks. Each week, take at least one step forward, no matter how small. Whether it's outlining your book, drafting your product idea, or creating a simple webpage—just move. As you progress, adjust your approach if needed, but keep pushing forward.

- **Step 5: Check In Weekly.** At the end of each week, revisit your progress. What's working? What needs to change? Don't get discouraged if things don't go exactly as planned. The key here is progress, not perfection. Make adjustments and keep going.

- **Step 6: Celebrate Your Growth.** After 48 days, celebrate what you've accomplished—whether it's finished or not.

This is a practice run, a way to build your confidence and momentum. Don't judge yourself on how perfect the outcome is; instead, focus on the fact that you took action and grew in the process.

Remember, this is just the beginning. You'll learn more specific ways to build income streams later in the book, but for now, it's about getting unstuck. It's about proving to yourself that you can take action, even when you don't feel fully ready. The goal is movement.

Key Takeaways:

- **Action comes before clarity**: You don't need to wait until you feel ready—progress happens when you take the first step. The 48-day timeline helps you build momentum by forcing quick decisions and action.

- **Start small, think big**: You can create multiple income streams from a single core message. Focus on repurposing your knowledge into different formats—books, courses, coaching, and more.

- **Perfection isn't the goal—movement is**: The 48-day action plan is about growth and progress, not getting everything perfect. The key is to start, adjust as you go, and celebrate the journey.

3
The Power of Teaching Frameworks

Simon Sinek wasn't an overnight success. He spent years trying to figure out why some companies seemed to inspire loyalty and thrive while others struggled. One day, he stumbled upon a simple idea. He realized that the most successful companies, like Apple and Southwest Airlines, didn't start by telling people what they did or how they did it. They started with why. They tapped into a purpose that resonated on a deep, emotional level. Sinek called this the "Golden Circle," a framework that placed *why* at the center of everything.

When Sinek first shared this idea, it was in a small, casual talk. But the power of his framework was undeniable. People could immediately understand it. It was simple, visual, and actionable. The Golden Circle wasn't just an abstract idea anymore. It became a roadmap for leaders to follow. From that one framework, Sinek's influence exploded. He made it a bestseller, a TED Talk with millions of views, and a sought-after consultant for top companies.[2]

That's the power of a framework. It simplifies complexity. It gives people a clear path to follow. When done right, a teaching framework becomes the backbone of everything you do—whether it's writing a book, giving a keynote, or designing a course. The clearer and more actionable your framework is, the easier it is for people to trust you as their guide. This chapter will show you why building a teaching framework is one of the most powerful things you can do to scale your message and your business.

Why Most Teaching Misses the Mark

Most people try to teach by dumping all their knowledge onto their audience at once. They share everything they know, thinking more information will lead to more understanding. But it doesn't. The truth is that people can't absorb that much at one time. It's overwhelming. They might nod along, but deep down, they're feeling lost, wondering how it all connects. This is what happens when there's no structure.

People want clarity. They want to know exactly how to get from point A to point B. When you throw too much at them, they end up doing nothing because they don't know where to start. It's not a lack of effort on their part—it's a lack of direction.

What most people need is a clear, simple path. They're looking for someone to break things down into steps, so they can feel confident taking action. This is where a teaching framework comes in. It's a map that shows them where they are, where they need to go, and how to get there.

Without a framework, your message gets lost in the noise. It might be valuable, but without structure, it's hard for people to see how it applies to them. When you create a clear framework, you give people a visual guide to success. And suddenly, everything clicks. They can see the big picture and understand the steps they need to take.

Instead of bombarding them with information, you're offering a clear path they can follow. It's like giving someone a GPS instead of just telling them to drive.

Steps for Building a Teaching Framework

Before I write a book, create a course, or launch a membership site, I take some time to create a teaching framework. It could be the old high school teacher in me, but I find it to be an effective tool. I'm honestly surprised more subject matter experts don't use this strategy. Like the image below, you'll find my teaching frameworks in almost anything I create.

Ready to create yours? Let's walk through the steps I take every time I design a new teaching framework.

Define the Transformation

It all starts with knowing what you're trying to accomplish. What's the end result you're helping people achieve? Maybe you're guiding them to build a business, or maybe it's a personal transformation like gaining confidence or improving their health. Whatever it is, you need to be crystal clear about the destination.

Without a defined transformation, your audience won't know what they're working toward. Think of it like trying to follow a trail without knowing where it leads. It's confusing and discouraging. Your job is to show them the end goal so they stay motivated.

As Stephen Covey said, "Begin with the end in mind." When you know where you're going, it's easier to create the steps that will get you there.

Identify the Key Milestones

Once you know the transformation, the next step is to break it down into key milestones. These are the big, essential steps that move someone closer to the end goal.

Think of these milestones as checkpoints. They're markers that tell people they're on the right track. Each one should represent a clear shift in progress. For example, if you're teaching someone how to start an online business, a milestone could be setting up their website. Another might be building an email list. Each milestone is a significant step forward.

Imagine building a house. You don't start with the roof. You begin with the foundation, then move on to the walls, and finally, the roof. Each step builds on the last, and that's exactly how your framework should work.

Create a Simple Visual Representation

A picture is worth a thousand words. When you take your framework and turn it into a visual, it becomes much easier for people to grasp. A one-page diagram can do more than a hundred paragraphs to explain your process.

Your visual should be simple enough that someone can understand it in seconds. Think of Donald Miller's StoryBrand framework. It's a straightforward story map that shows the journey from problem to success. It doesn't get more complicated than it needs to be.

Your framework doesn't have to be fancy. It could be a funnel, a roadmap, or a series of steps. What matters is that it's clear and easy to follow.

Use the Framework to Build Out Content

Once you've created your framework, it becomes the foundation for everything else. It's not just a diagram—it's the blueprint for your entire message. Your framework can guide the chapters of your book, the modules of your online course, or the main points of your keynote talk.

Each step of your framework can become a deep dive into its own section of content. If your framework has five steps, that's five chapters, five modules, or five lessons you can teach. This creates consistency and makes your message feel cohesive.

Think of your framework as the skeleton of a skyscraper. Each floor—the chapters, modules, or lessons—gets built on top of the same structure. It all works together to create something solid.

Test and Refine the Framework

Your framework isn't set in stone. In fact, it's a living tool that you can adjust over time. After you've used it in a few talks or worked through it with clients, you'll start to see what works and what doesn't.

Just like you'd test a bridge before letting cars cross, you need to test your framework. Run it by a small group, use it in a workshop, or try it out in a keynote speech. The feedback you get will help you refine it and make it stronger.

Jim Collins, author of *Good to Great*, said, "Good is the enemy of great." Your framework might be good at first, but with feedback and refining, it can become great. Don't be afraid to tweak and improve it as you go.

Today's Exercise: Create Your Teaching Framework

Here's a step-by-step exercise to help you create your own teaching framework.

First, write down the transformation you help people achieve. Be as specific as possible. Focus on the end result your audience will experience once they've followed your process.

Next, list three to seven key milestones that represent the major shifts your audience needs to make to achieve that transformation. Think of these as the essential steps that move them closer to the final goal.

Now, draw a simple visual representation of these milestones in sequence. This could be a diagram, a funnel, or even a roadmap—whatever feels natural for your process. Keep it clear and easy to follow.

Once you have your visual, use it as the foundation to outline the chapters of your book, the modules of your course, or the structure of your talks. Each milestone can serve as its own section, helping you build out your content with consistency.

Finally, test your framework with a small group or in a live setting. Gather feedback on whether it's easy to follow and where it might need improvement. Use this feedback to refine and strengthen your framework.

Key Takeaways:

- A good framework provides clarity. It simplifies complex ideas. This makes it easier for your audience to engage with your message.

- Your framework serves as the foundation for all your content—books, courses, coaching, and keynotes.

- A visual teaching tool builds your audience's trust in you. This leads to better results and stronger relationships.

4

Blueprint #1: The Hub and Spoke Income Method

What if I told you there was a smarter and faster way to share your message with the world? A way to turn a single idea into multiple income streams without feeling overwhelmed by constantly creating something new. For many bloggers and creators, the challenge isn't a good message. It's about using that message efficiently.

We often get caught up in the cycle of trying to create the next big thing, hoping it will finally take our business to the next level. But here's the reality: focusing on one product alone can lead to frustration. It's easy to feel like all the work, the marketing, and the promotion didn't yield the results we expected. So, what's the answer? Repurpose.

Instead of putting all your energy into one product, you can take that same core message and repurpose it into a variety of offerings. By doing this, you're no longer dependent on a single pathway to reach your audience. You're giving them multiple entry points to engage with your message, which opens the door to creating several streams of income at once.

I've experienced this firsthand. It all started with one idea—a book I was planning. But instead of just launching the book, I took a different approach. Over the course of twelve months, I turned that single message into seven distinct income streams. Let me take you back to the beginning.

How I Created Seven Income Streams in Twelve Months from One Message

The idea hit me in a Panera Bread. I was meeting with a coaching client who had driven two and a half hours just to spend a couple of hours with me. As he explained his business struggles, I had a realization. He wasn't just missing a product or two—he needed a whole framework.

"It sounds like you need an expert's product wheel," I said. Then, I grabbed a napkin and sketched out what would become the **Hub and Spoke Blueprint**.

Hub and Spoke Blueprint

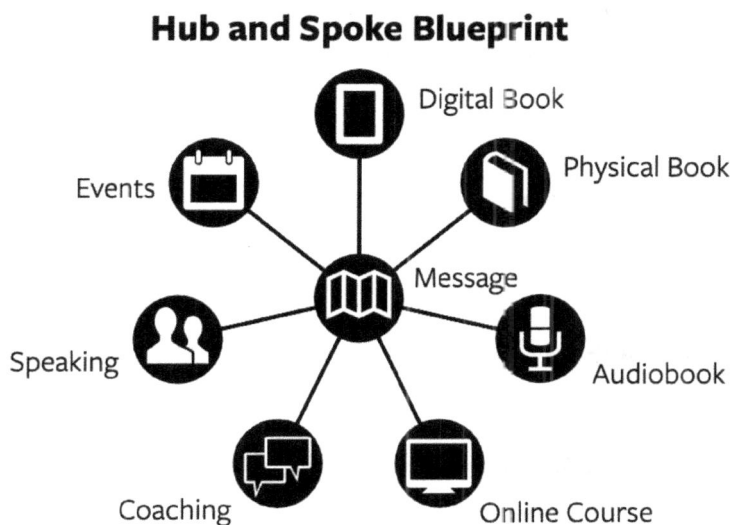

His core message was at the center of the diagram. Branching out from it were ways to deliver that message: events, speaking, coaching, a digital book, a physical book, an audiobook, and an online course. Each one was a potential income stream connected to the same core idea.

The simplicity of this model struck me. Not only did it offer multiple ways to reach people, but it also provided multiple ways to get paid for delivering the same message.

That day, as I explained this to my client, I realized I needed to do the exact same thing for my own business. I left Panera knowing I was sitting on a strategy that could completely transform my approach. At the time, I was working on a new book concept, but instead of treating it as a standalone project, I decided to make it the **hub** of a year-long plan. My goal? Create seven different income streams from that single message.

Here's how I did it:

- **Month 1:** I started by outlining the core message. This wasn't just a rough draft for a book; it was a roadmap for how I would teach, coach, and present that message across different platforms.

- **Months 2–4:** I wrote the first draft of my book. This was going to be the foundation, the piece that everything else would build from.

- **Month 5:** I launched the Kindle version of my book, creating my first income stream.

- **Month 6:** I followed it up with a self-published paperback version, establishing a second stream.

- **Month 7:** I narrated and released the audiobook on Amazon, iTunes, and Audible, which became the third income stream.

- **Month 8:** I crafted three keynote talks based on the book, which opened the door to speaking engagements and created my fourth income stream.

- **Month 9:** I launched a membership site tied to the book's principles, generating monthly recurring revenue—a fifth stream.

- **Month 10:** I rolled out a group coaching program, where participants could work through the book's content with my guidance, adding a sixth stream.

- **Month 12:** Finally, I hosted a live, high-end workshop, which became the seventh income stream and allowed me to teach my core message in person.

In just one year, I had created seven income streams from a single idea. And the beauty of it was that I wasn't constantly reinventing the wheel. I was simply repurposing one message into multiple formats, each tailored to a different part of my audience. Some people prefer books, others like to learn through courses or live events, and still others seek out one-on-one coaching. By offering all of these, I was able to maximize my reach and, more importantly, my revenue.

The Hub and Spoke Model

At the heart of scaling your income lies a simple but powerful concept: the **Hub and Spoke Model**. This framework lets you take your core message, the hub, and extend it into income-generating products and services, the spokes. Each spoke is a unique way to deliver the same message. It will reach different audience segments and create new revenue streams.

Imagine a wheel. The hub is your core message, the single most important idea that you want to share with the world. Whether you're a coach, author, speaker, or teacher, that core message is the foundation of everything you do. The spokes from the hub are the ways to deliver that message: books, courses, workshops, coaching sessions, keynote talks, membership sites, and more. These spokes don't just spread your message to a wider audience; they also provide multiple ways for you to get paid.

The genius of this model is its flexibility. You're not confined to one method of delivery. Instead, you're expanding your reach. You're using various platforms to suit different learning needs. Some people want to dive into a book, others prefer hands-on workshops, and still others seek out one-on-one coaching. By using the Hub and Spoke Model, you meet your audience where they are. You also give them many ways to engage with your message.

How the Hub and Spoke Framework Works

At the center of the Hub and Spoke framework is your **core message**. This is your central idea—the solution or transformation you offer to your audience. Your message doesn't change as it branches into various products or services. It's delivered through different formats, making it accessible in new ways.

Here's how it breaks down:

- **The Hub (Core Message):** This is the main idea you want to share with your audience. It could be your strategy to solve a problem, the framework you teach, or the principles you've created to help others achieve a goal. Think of the hub as the essential blueprint you've developed.

- **The Spokes (Income Streams):** Each spoke represents a

product, service, or platform that delivers your core message in a different way. For example:

- **Book**: A written version of your core message. This could be a self-published paperback, an eBook, or even an audiobook.

- **Online Course:** A deep dive into your message, in bite-sized lessons. They will guide people through your framework, step by step.

- **Workshops:** Virtual or in-person, they let participants interact with your message.

- **Membership Site:** A model where people pay for ongoing access to your content. It includes exclusive resources and personal coaching.

- **Speaking Engagements**: Keynote talks or seminars that allow you to spread your message on a larger stage.

- **1-on-1 Coaching:** A high-ticket offer. You provide personalized guidance to individuals seeking direct help with your framework.

- **Live Events**: Hosting events where attendees can engage deeply with your message and get personal access to you.

The Hub and Spoke Model is brilliant. Every spoke feeds back into the hub. This reinforces your core message and ensures consistency across platforms. You're not creating new messages; you're repurposing the same message in multiple ways.

Why the Hub and Spoke Model Works

The model works because it creates **multiple entry points** for your audience. Not everyone will come to you through the same path, and not everyone consumes content in the same way. Someone might discover you through your book, but another person may prefer the immersive experience of an online course. A third person could encounter your message at a keynote talk and later become a client for your high-end coaching program.

By offering your message in different formats, you give your audience options. More importantly, you create **multiple streams of income**—so you're not relying on one product to succeed. Each spoke supports the hub and reinforces the others, creating a steady and sustainable flow of revenue.

Adapting the Blueprint to Your Business

The Hub and Spoke Model is adaptable to any business or platform. It doesn't matter whether you're a writer, coach, speaker, or teacher—this framework can scale your message into multiple streams of income. Here's how you can visualize it:

- **Books:** Written content is often the easiest entry point. Your book becomes a lower-cost product that introduces your core message to a wider audience. From here, readers can ascend to higher-ticket offers like courses or coaching.

- **Courses:** For a structured, step-by-step approach, an online course is best. It offers a more in-depth learning experience. You can charge more for this kind of focused guidance.

- **Membership Sites:** A subscription model keeps your audience engaged long-term. It offers them ongoing access to new content, resources, or live coaching. This recurring revenue stream provides stability to your business.

- **Live Events and Workshops:** Some people learn best through direct interaction. Hosting workshops or live events engages your audience in real-time. It also lets you charge more for these in-depth experiences.

- **Coaching:** 1-on-1 or group coaching lets you work directly with clients who need personalized attention. This high-end service can transform your most engaged followers into loyal clients.

The Hub and Spoke Model lets you scale your business, create multiple income streams, and—most importantly—reach people in the best way for them. You're amplifying the impact of your message while building a sustainable, scalable business.

Today's Exercise: Create Your Own Hub and Spoke Blueprint

Now that you understand the power of the Hub and Spoke Model, it's time to put it into action. This exercise will help you map your core message. It will also help you brainstorm income streams. Use these to start building your hub and spoke framework. Grab a notebook or open a new document, and let's get started.

Step 1: Identify Your Core Message (The Hub)

Before you can build out your spokes, you need to define the core idea that will sit at the center of your business. This is the foundation of your message—the solution, framework, or method you offer.

Think about your area of expertise, the problem you solve, or the transformation you provide.

- **Question to Answer:** What is the key message or framework you want to share with your audience?

  - Example: "I help entrepreneurs turn their expertise into multiple streams of income."

Write down your core message in one clear, concise sentence. This will be your hub.

Step 2: Brainstorm Your Spokes (Income Streams)

Now that you have your core message, it's time to brainstorm the different ways you can deliver it to your audience. Remember, each spoke is a product or service that repurposes your core message. Don't limit yourself—think about various platforms, formats, and delivery methods.

- **Question to Answer:** How can you turn your core message into different products or services?

Here are some ideas to consider:

- **Book:** Could you write a book to introduce your core message to a wider audience?

- **Online Course:** Could you break down your message into step-by-step lessons?

- **Workshops:** Would your audience benefit from live workshops, either virtual or in-person?

- **Coaching:** Can you offer personalized coaching or group sessions to provide hands-on guidance?

- **Membership Site:** Could you build a membership site for ongoing access to exclusive content and resources?

- **Speaking:** Are there opportunities to deliver your message as a keynote speaker at events or conferences?

- **Live Events:** Could you host a seminar, retreat, or live training event?

Write down all the potential income streams you can think of, using the core message as the foundation for each one.

Step 3: Prioritize and Create a Timeline

Once you've brainstormed your list of potential income streams, the next step is to prioritize them. Which ones feel most natural for you to start with? Which could be launched quickly, and which might take more time to develop?

- **Question to Answer:** What income streams can you realistically create in the next 3 to 12 months?

Organize your spokes in order of priority. For example:

1. Write and launch a book.

2. Develop an online course.

3. Create a membership site for ongoing support.

Now, create a simple timeline. For each spoke, assign a deadline based on when you plan to launch it. Don't overwhelm yourself by trying to launch everything at once—start with one or two and build from there.

Step 4: Take Action

Now that you have your core message, your list of potential income streams, and a timeline for launching them, it's time to take action. Your goal for this week is to complete the first step toward creating your initial income stream.

- **Action Step:** Pick one spoke from your list and commit to working on it this week. Whether it's outlining your book, drafting your course modules, or mapping out your membership site, take that first step.

At the end of the week, evaluate your progress and set your next goal. To scale your message, act consistently. Each step creates income streams that support your core message.

Step 5: Reflect and Adjust

As you work through this process, keep in mind that the Hub and Spoke Model is flexible. You can always adjust your plan as you learn what resonates with your audience. After launching your first product, reflect on the feedback you receive. Is there a different format your audience is asking for? Should you shift the order of your spokes based on demand?

- **Question to Answer:** What have you learned from launching your first spoke, and how can you apply that to the next one?

Use these insights to fine-tune your blueprint as you continue to build out your income streams.

By the end, you will have mapped your Hub and Spoke Blueprint, found income streams, and begun scaling your message. Remember, the key is to start with one spoke, launch it, and then move on to the next. This steady, strategic approach will help grow your business. It will also amplify your core message's impact.

Key Takeaways:

- Repurpose your message into multiple income streams with books, courses, coaching, and more.

- Offer different ways for your audience to engage, meeting them where they are.

- Scale smartly by adapting one core idea rather than constantly creating new content.

5

Blueprint #2: The Rapid Validation Income Method

When Dave Thomas opened the first Wendy's in 1969, he didn't do what most fast-food chains were doing. Instead of offering a sprawling menu of options, he stripped it down to five simple items: hamburgers, fries, soda, chili, and the Frosty. It was a bold move, especially in an industry that thrived on variety. But this minimalist approach wasn't just about making food faster—it was a test. By narrowing the focus, Wendy's could gauge what people really wanted.

The Frosty, a thick and creamy dessert, became an instant hit. That wasn't by accident. Thomas didn't overwhelm his customers with too many choices. He offered only the essentials, creating a clear path to see what resonated most. The simplicity made it easier to tweak the menu, improve quality, and optimize service. Wendy's bet on this small, focused menu paid off. They validated what worked and then scaled. That's why, decades later, it's still one of the biggest names in fast food.[3]

The same principle applies to building a business or product. You don't need to have it all figured out from day one. You just need something simple—something that lets you test, improve, and grow. That's where the *Rapid Validation Income Method* comes in. Like Wendy's Frosty, it's about offering a small, manageable product first, learning from your audience, and then expanding. It's how you build confidence, save time, and avoid costly mistakes.

The Four Validation Offer Types

Validation offers are the simplest way to test your ideas without a huge upfront investment. They're designed to be easy to create, sell, and adjust based on feedback. These offers help you understand what your audience truly wants. The goal isn't to perfect the product but to put it in front of real people and see how they respond.

Mini

Writer	Low-Content Book
Teacher	Mini-Course
Speaker	Paid Virtual Workshop
Coach	4-Week Group Coaching

The first type is a **Low-Content Book**. This works well for writers. It's a book that doesn't require a lot of writing, like a workbook, journal, or planner. It's straightforward to create, and readers love practical tools they can use right away.

For teachers or educators, the **Mini-Course** is ideal. It's a short online course that breaks down a topic into a few digestible lessons. You don't need to cover everything—just enough to provide value and get people interested.

Speakers thrive with a *Paid Virtual Workshop*. This is a live, interactive session where you teach, engage, and answer questions in real-time. It's perfect for testing a new idea because you get instant feedback from your audience.

Coaches can offer a *4-Week Bootcamp*. This is a group coaching experience that takes place over a month, with weekly sessions. It's a hands-on way to help your audience get results, while also building deeper connections with them.

Each validation offer lets you test your concept quickly. You can get feedback and improve it, all before wasting time or money. The beauty of these offers is that they're flexible and easy to adjust based on what you learn.

Model 1. Single Format, Multi-Offer

In this model, you stick to one validation offer format—like virtual workshops—and use it to offer different topics over time. The idea is to master a single format that works well for you and your audience, then consistently use that format to teach new, related topics. This approach lets you focus on refining one method of delivery while keeping your content fresh and engaging.

For example, if you're a speaker, you could run virtual workshops throughout the year. Each workshop tackles a different subject, but the structure and delivery stay the same. This consistency builds trust. Your audience knows what to expect from your workshops. But, the changing topics keep them engaged and eager to learn more.

Here's how a year of virtual workshops might look:

- Workshop 1: "Building Your Brand Foundation" - A 90-minute session on the basics of building a strong personal or business brand.

- Workshop 2: "Creating a Content Strategy That Converts" – A guide to planning and organizing content that boosts engagement and leads.

- Workshop 3: "Monetizing Your Digital Products" - Steps to turn digital content into revenue.

- Workshop 4: "Scaling Your Online Business with Automation" - A guide to using automation tools to grow your business without burning out.

Each workshop offers a new topic, but the delivery method stays consistent. This simplifies the process for you and helps your audience get comfortable with your teaching style. Don't reinvent the wheel every time. Instead, master one format. Then, deliver consistent value across different subjects.

The same is true with the other three validation offers. For example:

- Low-Content Book: Create and launch four or more books in a year to see what resonates most with your audience.

- Mini-Course: Record and launch four or more mini-courses on the hottest topics in your niche. You can expand it into a flagship course based on which one sells best.

- 4-Week Bootcamp: Every 90 days, launch another 4-week bootcamp with a different topic focus.

This model lets you streamline your process. It offers variety, keeps your audience engaged, and builds loyalty over time.

Model 2. Single Topic, Multi-Offer

This approach takes one topic and turns it into various formats. It offers your audience different ways to engage with the same idea. It lets you explore a topic in depth. It offers options for people to learn based on their preferences and styles. The topic stays consistent, but the formats change to fit different needs.

Let's say your main topic is "Building an Email List." You could create several types of offers that revolve around this theme, but each format would serve a different audience. This makes your content more accessible and appealing to a wider audience. You won't need to create new ideas for each offer.

Here's how this might look:

- Low-Content Book: A workbook of email templates, checklists, and planning tools. They help your audience quickly set up their first email campaign.

- Paid Virtual Workshop: A live, interactive session that walks participants step-by-step through setting up an email funnel, with Q&A time at the end.

- Mini-Course: A self-paced course with videos. They break down the email-building process into simple, easy steps.

- 4-Week Bootcamp: A hands-on coaching program. You will work with a small group. Along the way, you offer personal feedback and guidance as they build and grow their email lists.

Each offer taps into the same topic but presents it in a way that caters to different learning preferences. The workbook gives tools. The workshop provides live teaching. The mini-course allows self-paced learning. The boot camp offers accountability and support.

This model lets you meet diverse needs while staying on one topic. It helps you repurpose content and grow your audience without overextending yourself.

Model 3. Multi-Topics, Multi-Offer

In the Multi-Topics, Multi-Offer Model, you create various offers in different formats. Each offer targets a niche within a broader subject. This approach lets you speak to subgroups in your audience. It tailors your content to their specific needs and interests, while staying in the same area of expertise.

This model works well if you serve a diverse audience that needs different solutions based on their role or focus. You create multiple offers for each niche. You use different formats to connect with the right people at the right time. The key is that while the formats vary, each offer focuses on a specific audience within the larger topic.

For example, let's say your broader topic is *Content Marketing.* You could create different offers aimed at specific groups within that space:

- Low-Content Book for Bloggers: A workbook for creating shareable blog posts. It offers templates for blog planning, keyword research, and social media promotion.

- Paid Virtual Workshop for YouTubers: A live session on optimizing videos for engagement and growth. It will cover tips for thumbnails, titles, and video SEO.

- Mini-Course for Podcasters: A short course on boosting

podcast downloads. It covers content structuring, episode marketing, and audience engagement strategies.

- 4-Week Bootcamp for Social Media Influencers: A group coaching program focused on social media growth. It helps influencers build a brand and grow their audience with targeted content.

Each offer targets a niche. It lets you serve bloggers, YouTubers, podcasters, and influencers without spreading yourself too thin. The low-content book provides quick tools for bloggers. The workshop delivers live, hands-on help for YouTubers. The mini-course offers step-by-step lessons for podcasters. The boot camp gives influencers long-term, personalized guidance.

This model lets you reach multiple audiences in the same field. It gives you the flexibility to address their needs and diversify your income. By addressing each niche with a tailored offer, you can deepen your connection with different segments of your market.

Which Model is Right for You?

Choosing the right model depends on two key factors: your strengths and your audience's preferences. The right fit will help you create offers that are not only easier for you to deliver but also more engaging for your audience. Each model has its advantages. But, you must choose the one that fits your natural talents and your audience's learning preferences.

Start by evaluating your strengths. If you thrive in a live environment and enjoy real-time interaction, the Single Format, Multi-Offer Model might be perfect for you. You can focus on running virtual workshops or live events, sticking to a format that plays to your strengths. The consistency will help you refine your delivery. Your audience will know what to expect each time you release something new.

If you prefer variety and love the idea of creating different formats around a single topic, the Single Topic, Multi-Offer Model is a good choice. This lets you offer a mix of content, from books to courses to bootcamps, all centered around one subject. It's perfect if you enjoy working with different types of media and want to reach different learners.

The Multi-Topics, Multi-Offer Model is ideal if you serve diverse subgroups within a larger audience. If your market has distinct niches, you can create highly targeted offers that speak to each one. This model allows you to meet a variety of needs while still staying focused on your core expertise.

When considering your audience's preferences, think about how they like to learn. Do they prefer self-paced content, or do they engage more with live, interactive experiences? Do they need step-by-step guidance over time, or do they want quick, actionable tools they can use right away? Understanding their needs will help you decide whether to focus on workshops, courses, books, or coaching programs.

The best model is the one that lets you deliver your content naturally. It should help you connect with your audience and build a lasting business. It's about using your strengths. Meet your audience where they are. Then, deliver value and grow with confidence.

Today's Exercise: Choose Your Rapid Validation Model

This exercise will help you identify which validation model best suits your strengths and your audience's needs. Take 20-30 minutes to reflect and jot down your answers. By the end, you'll have a clearer idea of which model you should focus on to test and grow your offers.

Step 1: Evaluate Your Strengths

Think about what comes naturally to you. Are you more comfortable creating live, interactive experiences? Do you prefer pre-recorded content? Do you enjoy creating hands-on tools or written resources?

- Write down your top three strengths when it comes to teaching or presenting information. Examples might include live speaking, writing, creating videos, or coaching.

- Now, reflect on the formats you enjoy the most. Would you rather run a live workshop, write a book, or guide a small group over time? List your preferred formats.

Example:

- Strengths: Speaking, engaging with live audiences, and answering questions on the spot.

- Preferred format: Virtual workshops or boot camps.

Step 2: Understand Your Audience's Learning Preferences

Consider how your audience prefers to learn. Do they like to learn at their own pace, or do they want hands-on guidance? Are they looking for a quick solution, or are they seeking in-depth support over time?

- Write down what you know about your audience's learning preferences. Are they busy professionals who need quick, actionable advice? Or are they learners who value long-term support and accountability?

- List the types of content your audience responds to the most. Is it live interaction, step-by-step video lessons, workbooks, or personalized coaching?

Example:

- Audience: Busy entrepreneurs who want quick, actionable tips and enjoy live Q&As.

- Popular content: Live workshops, short courses.

Step 3: Choose Your Model

Based on your strengths and your audience's preferences, decide which validation model aligns best with both. Use the notes from Steps 1 and 2 to guide your choice.

If you excel in a single format and your audience values consistency, the Single Format, Multi-Offer Model might suit you. You could create a series of virtual workshops or courses around different topics within your niche.

If you like creating various formats for a diverse audience, use the Single Topic, Multi-Offer Model. It lets you meet different needs with a workbook, a course, and a bootcamp, all on one core topic.

For a diverse audience with different sub-niches, use the Multi-Topics, Multi-Offer Model. It is a great choice. You could create different offers for each group, like a book for beginners and a workshop for more advanced learners.

Step 4: Brainstorm Your First Offer

Now, brainstorm the first validation offer you'll create based on your chosen model. Keep it simple. What's a topic you know well that aligns with your audience's biggest pain points or needs? Decide on a format that suits both you and your audience.

- Write down the first offer you'll create.

- Include the format, topic, and a brief description of the value it provides.

Example:

- Format: Paid virtual workshop.

- Topic: "How to Build a Powerful Personal Brand in 90 Minutes."

- Description: A live, interactive workshop. It will teach step-by-step strategies for creating a personal brand. There will be a Q&A at the end.

Step 5: Set Your Timeline

Set a realistic timeline to create and launch your first offer. Give yourself a deadline for completion, and outline the steps you'll take to get there.

- Write down your target launch date.

- List the key steps you'll need to take (e.g., planning content, setting up a registration page, marketing the offer).

Example:

- Launch date: 48 days from today.

- Steps: Plan the content outline, set up the event page, and start promoting the workshop via email and social media.

By the end of this exercise, you'll have a clear direction on which model suits you, what offer to create, and a plan to bring it to life. This is the first step toward building a scalable, validated income stream.

Key Takeaways:

- Create simple, quick-to-launch validation offers. Test what resonates with your audience.

- Choose the validation model that aligns with your strengths and fits how your audience prefers to learn.

- Use quick feedback from your first offer to improve and scale, avoiding wasted time and effort.

6

Blueprint #3: The Max Velocity Income Method

Think back to why you started your entrepreneurial journey in the first place. For most of us, it's the same dream: freedom, flexibility, and financial independence. The idea of owning your time, being in control of your income, and having the space to enjoy life on your terms. No more being tied to a desk, clocking in and out, or answering to someone else's vision. It's your business, your dream, and your chance to build something meaningful.

But as your business grew, you might have realized that freedom wasn't as easy to come by as you imagined. Instead of enjoying flexibility, you found yourself tied to the grind—working more hours than ever before. Trading time for money became your norm, and the hustle never seemed to stop. If you weren't chasing the next sale or launching the next offer, your income took a hit. The dream of freedom felt further away than ever as you got stuck in the cycle of feast or famine.

Sound familiar?

Now, imagine a different scenario. What if you could break free from that exhausting pattern? What if your business made money without your constant attention? It could keep earning, even while you took time off or worked on other projects. What if there was a system that allowed you to *finally* enjoy the freedom you set out to achieve?

That's exactly what the Max Velocity Income Method is designed to do.

This method aims to build a high-revenue business. It does so through recurring income streams. It avoids trading hours for dollars or hustling for every sale. It's about creating a system that works for you, not the other way around.

Use three income streams: book royalties, a membership site, and high-value coaching memberships. This will create a reliable, predictable revenue system. This method allows you to scale without burning out, so you can finally experience the freedom and flexibility you've been working toward.

The Max Velocity Income Method isn't about quick fixes or shortcuts. It's a strategy that requires upfront effort and planning, but the payoff is enormous. Once it's in place, your income will flow in automatically, month after month. It will free you from the constant chase and give you stability. You can then grow your business with confidence.

So, if you're tired of the grind and ready to take control of your business—and your life—this is your path forward. Let's dive into how the Max Velocity Income Method can transform the way you earn and finally give you the freedom you've been striving for.

The Max Velocity Income Method Explained

The Max Velocity Income Method is for those ready to invest time and effort in building a high-revenue, sustainable business. While it's the most complex and time-consuming strategy in this book, it offers the highest income potential. The method revolves around leveraging recurring revenue streams, which provide stability and predictability.

The key focus of this method is the *Max Offers* column of the Messenger Product Map. These high-tier offers require more setup but yield significant long-term returns.

Max

The model operates on three main recurring revenue streams:

- **Book Royalties**: Monthly royalties from Amazon create a steady stream of passive income. With multiple books, the income compounds and becomes a reliable foundation for your business.

- **Membership Site**: A subscription-based site where members pay a monthly fee for access to exclusive content. This provides ongoing, scalable revenue at an affordable price point.

- **Coaching Membership:** The top access level. Members pay a premium for personalized coaching. This is your best offer. It will generate high, recurring revenue through deeper, one-on-one engagement.

These three streams allow you to build a business where income is consistent, reducing the need to chase constant new sales. Focusing on Max Offers creates a system. It allows revenue to grow predictably over time. This lets you focus on creating value, not on cash flow.

The Customer Journey of the Max Velocity Income Method

Customer Stage 1. Buy Your Book(s)

A book series acts as the gateway into your entire system. It's the first point of contact where readers discover your message, and it introduces them to your ecosystem. The key here isn't just to write a single book but to create a series that allows you to stay in front of your audience over time. Each book serves as an entry point that can turn casual readers into long-term customers.

Lead magnets are essential for each book. A lead magnet is a free resource offered to readers in exchange for their email addresses. These offers, placed inside your books, turn readers into subscribers. Once they opt-in, you've opened the door to a deeper relationship through email, which can then guide them into your membership or coaching offers.

Shorter books work better in this system. Traditional nonfiction books can be 60,000 words or more. But, for the Max Velocity Income Method, shorter books (around 30,000 words) are better. These books are quicker to produce, easier for readers to consume, and can be released more frequently, which keeps your name and brand top of mind. Focusing on compact, actionable content will build momentum. It will also increase potential entry points into your ecosystem.

Customer Stage 2. Opt-in to Your Email List

Once you've captured a reader's email, the next step is nurturing that relationship through email sequences. Email is your tool for building trust and demonstrating value over time. It's not just about selling; it's about providing consistent, helpful content that speaks to your audience's needs and interests.

An email sequence allows you to guide your subscribers on a journey. You start by offering free resources, tips, and insights related to the topics covered in your book. This consistent communication builds rapport and keeps you on their radar. Over time, you can introduce them to your membership site and invite them to take the next step with you.

The goal is to establish trust first. By giving away value before asking for anything, you build goodwill. Once your readers see you as a reliable and helpful resource, they'll be more likely to explore your paid offerings when the time comes.

Customer Stage 3. Join Your Membership Site

A membership site is the next step in scaling your income. Structuring a membership site allows you to offer valuable content on a recurring basis for a monthly or annual fee. The membership site is where readers can dive deeper into your teachings, access exclusive content, and engage with a community of like-minded people.

Membership sites differ from coaching memberships in two key ways: price and access. A membership site is typically more affordable, with prices ranging from $20 to $100 per month. It offers access to resources but not direct, one-on-one engagement. Members get valuable content but won't have direct interaction with you in most cases.

This structure makes membership sites scalable. You can serve a large audience without having to invest significant amounts of personal time. It also allows people to test out your materials and see if they're ready for more in-depth involvement, like upgrading to a coaching membership.

Customer Stage 4. Upgrade to Your Coaching Membership

Coaching memberships are where the highest level of access and revenue comes in. A coaching membership is different from a membership site. It offers personalized support and direct engagement with you. This might include weekly calls, personalized feedback, or one-on-one mentoring. The price point is higher, typically ranging from $200 to $1,000 per month, depending on the level of access and services provided.

The value of the coaching membership lies in the personal connection. Subscribers are not just paying for content—they're paying for your expertise, guidance, and time. This creates a higher level of commitment from your clients, and in return, they get deeper, more personalized results.

Offering an upgrade from the membership site to the coaching membership is a natural progression. As members engage with your content and see value, some will want more. You create a new revenue stream by offering a clear path for those ready to invest at a higher level. This also adds more value for your most committed followers.

How to Build Your Max Velocity Income Method

When setting up the Max Velocity Income Method, the process doesn't start where you might expect. Instead of starting with your most accessible offer, you build your system from the back. You start with your highest-value offer—your coaching membership—and work toward more accessible entry points. This reverse approach ensures that the foundation of your business is solid, and each step builds on the next.

Step 1. Launch the Coaching Membership

The first step is to focus on your coaching membership. Even with a small group of 5 to 10 members, this is where you can make the biggest impact early on. Working closely with a few committed clients creates great value. You also learn from them. You'll quickly discover their struggles, goals, and what they need from you. This direct feedback is invaluable for refining your teaching framework.

Instead of guessing what your audience wants, the coaching membership lets you test and iterate in real time. The insights you gain here will shape the content and strategies you use as you expand into other areas. The beauty of starting with coaching is its personal nature. It lets you build deep relationships and test your methods before scaling them to a wider audience.

Step 2. Launch Your Membership Site

Once your coaching membership is up and running, the next step is to create a more affordable option for those who aren't ready to invest in coaching. A membership site provides ongoing value but at a lower price point. It offers valuable content, like lessons and tutorials. It includes community engagement but lacks one-on-one coaching interaction.

This membership site becomes the middle tier in your system. For those who aren't ready or able to commit to the coaching membership, it offers a way to engage with your material at a more comfortable level. It also acts as a funnel. It lets members see your value. They may upgrade to the coaching membership when they want more.

By offering this lower-cost option, you create a scalable source of recurring income. The membership site allows you to serve a larger audience while maintaining a lighter personal workload.

Step 3. Write Your Book Series

The final piece of the system is your book series. Books serve as the ultimate lead-generation tool. By writing and releasing books regularly, you create multiple entry points for new leads to discover you. Each book can share your message and invite readers to join your email list. This connects them to your membership site and coaching offerings.

The key to success with the book series is consistency. Focus on releasing shorter, manageable books on a regular schedule. These 30,000-word books are quicker to produce, easier for readers to digest, and they keep your name visible. Each book builds on the last, feeding the overall system by continuously bringing in new leads.

A book series isn't just a way to share your expertise—it's a gateway into your entire system. Readers find your books, join your list, and learn about your membership and coaching. This reverse approach, starting with the coaching, then the books, ensures your business is built to grow and scale.

Today's Exercise: Build Your Max Velocity Income Map

This exercise will help you start your Max Velocity Income system. It focuses on three key steps: launching your coaching membership, creating your membership site, and writing your book series. Follow these steps to map out your plan and start taking action.

Step 1: Define Your Coaching Membership

- Think about the core problem or challenge your target audience faces. Write it down.

- Outline how your coaching membership will solve that problem. What kind of personalized support will you offer? Will you hold weekly calls, provide one-on-one guidance, or give tailored feedback? Be specific.

- Write down the specific outcome your coaching members will achieve after working with you. Make this outcome clear and measurable.

- Set a pricing model for your coaching membership. Consider offering a small group program to start, with just 5 to 10 members. Write down your ideal price per member.

Step 2: Map Out Your Membership Site

- Outline the core content or resources you'll offer in your membership site. This could include video lessons, worksheets, templates, or access to a community forum.

- Write down 3 to 5 pieces of content you could create today to populate the membership site.

- Determine the pricing for your membership site. This should be lower than the coaching membership, so it's accessible to more people. Write down your membership site's price per month.

- Plan an introductory offer for people who join your membership site. What bonus or discount could you offer to encourage sign-ups?

Step 3: Brainstorm Your Book Series

- Identify the overarching theme for your book series. What is the core message that ties all the books together? Write this theme down.

- Brainstorm 3 to 5 book topics that align with this theme. Each book should solve a specific problem or answer a key question for your audience. Write down potential titles or concepts for each book.

- Plan a timeline for writing and releasing these books. Start with a shorter book of about 30,000 words. Write down your goal for completing the first draft of the book.

Final Task: Create Your Max Velocity Map

- On a blank sheet of paper or document, map out your Max Velocity Income system. Start with the coaching membership at the center. Add your membership site as a step below that and the book series as the entry point.

- Use arrows to show how each step feeds into the next. For example, books lead to email list sign-ups, which lead to membership offers, which can then lead to coaching upgrades.

- Look at your map. What's the first action you can take today to begin building this system? Write it down and commit to doing it.

This exercise will give you a clear plan. It will show you how to build a recurring revenue system from back to front. This will lay the foundation for long-term success.

Key Takeaways:

- Build your system from the back. Start with high-value coaching memberships. Then, scale down to more affordable options.

- Leverage shorter, actionable books as entry points to attract new leads and guide them into your ecosystem.

- Focus on recurring revenue, like book royalties and coaching. This will create stable, predictable income.

7

Blueprint #4: The Price Pyramid Income Method

I t was May of 2022, and I knew something had to change. For the past decade, my main sales strategy was webinars. Free training sessions that would hopefully lead to sales at the end. And for a while, it worked. People showed up, a percentage bought my course or coaching program, and the cycle repeated. But over time, I noticed a shift. The method started feeling worn out.

Too many in my niche were doing the same thing. Their webinars had become predictable. They were just long sales pitches disguised as free training. They offered little value upfront. Most promised to send out recordings, which only made people less likely to show up live. Attendance rates dropped, and even when people did show up, they were disengaged. It felt like the magic of webinars had fizzled out.

That's when I decided to pivot. Instead of offering another free webinar, I decided to charge a small fee for people to attend a workshop. The price point wasn't high—somewhere between $25 and $45—but the effect was immediate and powerful. One hundred people paid $25 each to attend that first workshop. Just like that, I made $2,500 before even creating the workshop slides.

But the real insight came during the workshop itself. Those who paid to attend were more engaged. They weren't there to coast through a free session—they were invested. The energy shifted. People asked more questions, took more notes, and were eager to learn. By the time I made my offer for a four-week group coaching program, they were ready to act.

That small fee changed everything. It made people value the experience more, which in turn boosted the results of my sales offers. The workshop wasn't just a paid entry—it became a stepping stone to bigger, more meaningful offers. The Price Pyramid Income Method was born. A low-cost workshop led to high-level coaching and ongoing memberships.

In this chapter, I'll show you exactly how this method works and why it's a game-changer for scaling your income.

Why Most Webinars Fail

Most entrepreneurs mistakenly jump to high-ticket offers. They expect some free webinar attendees to convert into paying customers. The typical approach is a long, free webinar or sales presentation, packed with content but designed to lead to a big offer at the end. The problem is, more often than not, this model falls flat.

People tune out when they feel like they're sitting through a sales pitch disguised as free content. They came for value, but what they get is a drawn-out sales presentation. That's where the engagement drops off. Free attendees don't feel committed. They may watch passively or only half-listen, knowing they haven't invested anything. And if they're not invested, they're not engaged. When it comes time to make the offer, the results are predictable: low conversions and poor sales.

Free attendees, while plentiful, are often less committed. They don't have any skin in the game, which means they don't take it as seriously. They may show up, but they're distracted, waiting for the catch.

And when they sense that the whole session is one big sales push, they mentally check out.

There's also a trust gap. Jumping from a free webinar to a high-ticket offer feels like too big of a leap for many. A big financial investment, without building trust, creates resistance. The audience isn't primed for such a big ask, and it shows in the conversion numbers.

The Price Pyramid Income Method flips this model on its head. Instead of starting with free, begin with a low-priced, high-value offer. Think of it as a small, paid workshop that delivers real, actionable insights. It draws in committed attendees—those who are willing to pay for value.

As you deliver genuine value at that first level, you're building trust and engagement. Each offer leads to the next. It starts with a low-ticket workshop. Then, a more intensive implementation offer. Finally, a high-level coaching program. By the time your audience reaches the top of the pyramid, they're ready. They've seen the value, they trust the process, and they're eager for more. This method boosts conversion rates. It also builds loyal clients who feel they're climbing a valuable ladder.

How to Implement the Price Pyramid Income Method

The Price Pyramid Income Method has nothing to do with a pyramid scheme. It's called the Price Pyramid Income Method because of the number of people and the price points between offers. For example:

- **The bottom of the pyramid** has the highest number of conversions and the lowest price point. This offer attracts the most people because it's affordable and requires minimal commitment. It's the broadest part of your funnel.

- **The middle of the pyramid** is more expensive and requires a moderate time commitment. Fewer people will move to this level, but those who do are more invested in learning and applying what you teach.

- **The top of the pyramid** is the narrowest, representing a small percentage of highly committed individuals. They are ready to invest in your highest-tier program. They've seen the value and want deeper, personalized support.

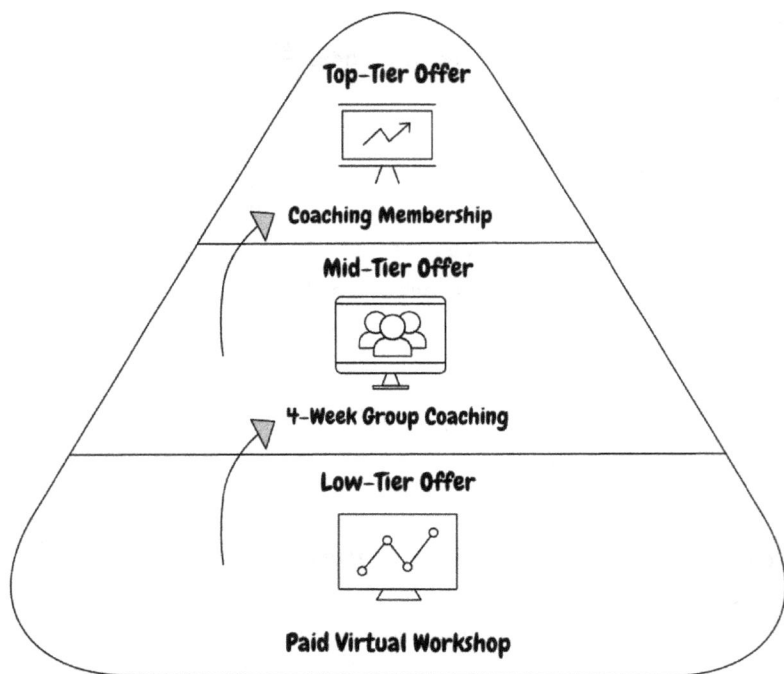

The Price Pyramid Income Method isn't about gimmicks or schemes. It's named for the natural flow between pricing and participation. At the bottom, you have the largest group of people engaging with your most affordable offer. As you move up, the commitment—both financially and in time—grows, but so does the value you deliver.

By the time you reach the top, only a small, highly committed group remains. These individuals have journeyed with you through each step, seen the results, and are now ready for your highest-level support. This approach builds trust, maximizes engagement, and leads to sustainable income growth. Let's explore how to set up your own Price Pyramid Income Method.

Step 1: Run a Paid Virtual Workshop

The foundation of the Price Pyramid begins with a paid workshop. Instead of offering free content, charge a small fee to attend live training. This creates a filter that attracts people who are serious about learning. They've paid to be there, which means they're already invested, even if the fee is modest.

Charging $25-$45 for a workshop has a powerful effect. First, it increases your show-up rate. People who pay are far more likely to actually attend because they've already committed financially. Once they show up, they're engaged and paying attention. You've created a stronger relationship with them just by asking for a small investment. They're more open to learning and more likely to follow through on what you teach. That initial buy-in sets the stage for deeper engagement as you move them through your sales funnel.

Step 2: Choose Your Implementation Offer

Once the workshop is over, the next step is to offer participants a way to put their new knowledge into action. This is where the implementation offer comes into play. The goal here is to help them apply what they've learned in a structured, supportive environment.

Popular offers include a four-week group coaching boot camp, one-on-one coaching, or access to a membership. The key is to make it practical and action-oriented. Your audience needs to feel like they're not just learning but actually moving forward. A well-done step creates a bridge between theory and practice. It gives people the tools to apply your teachings in their lives. It's about helping them achieve real results, not just delivering information. They leave this phase feeling like they've accomplished something, which makes them more open to future offers.

Step 3: Decide Your Upgrade Offer

The final step is to offer an ongoing or higher-level service. At this point, your audience has gone through the workshop and the implementation phase. They've seen the value of what you offer and have begun to make progress. Now, they're primed for the next level.

This could be one-on-one coaching or a membership that gives them continued access to you and your resources. The upgrade offer should feel like a natural extension of the implementation phase. For example, if your audience just finished a four-week boot camp, it makes sense to offer them a membership for continued coaching and support. They're already in the mindset of growth and learning, and your offer gives them a way to keep that momentum going. It feels like the next logical step, not a hard sell because it directly ties into the progress they've already made.

Today's Exercise: Build Your Price Pyramid

Step 1: Choose a topic you're passionate about teaching.

This should be something that aligns with your expertise and solves a problem your audience cares about. Create a simple outline for a live paid workshop. Focus on delivering clear, actionable value in a 60-90 minute session.

Step 2: Set the price for your workshop.

Aim for a range between $25 and $45. This price is low enough to attract a wide audience but high enough to ensure participants are committed. Once you've decided, start promoting it to your audience through email, social media, or any platform you use to connect with them.

Step 3: Develop your implementation offer.

Think about how you can help your workshop attendees take action on what they've learned. A four-week group coaching program is a great option, but it could also be a one-on-one session or a membership site. The key is to provide hands-on support to guide them through applying what they've learned from the workshop.

Step 4: Create a high-ticket coaching offer to follow the implementation phase.

This could be a monthly membership for ongoing coaching. Or a more personalized one-on-one coaching package. The goal is to continue supporting your participants on their journey, offering them more value as they move up your pyramid.

Key Takeaways:

- Start with a low-priced, high-value offer to engage and build trust with your audience.

- Gradually introduce mid-tier and high-tier offers to those who are more committed and ready for deeper support.

- The Price Pyramid Income Method lets you grow your income. It does this while nurturing long-term client relationships.

8

Blueprint #5: The Single Lane Income Method

Back in 2011, I launched BloggingYourPassion.com. I'd already built a successful blog around career coaching, tapping into different income streams along the way. However, I wanted to shift gears to teach others how to navigate the online world of marketing and audience building.

I knew one thing: I'm a teacher at heart. So, when I started this new brand, I didn't dive into everything at once. Instead, I kept it simple. My first product was a mini course called Blogging Your Passion University 101. The goal was straightforward—help people set up a blog the right way. I put it out there, and the sales started rolling in.

That's when it hit me. The power of starting small and working within one lane. I soon created a flagship course. It had levels 101, 201, 301, and 401. They covered everything from blogging to traffic generation to earning income online. The flagship course became known as Blogging Your Passion University.

And finally, two years later, I transitioned to a monthly membership model. Instead of offering a one-time payment, I was now receiving monthly recurring revenue to teach what I love. The whole thing unfolded naturally, and it worked because I stayed in my lane. I kept things focused on teaching, growing my offers step by step.

I didn't call it this at the time, but I was following what I now call the **Single Lane Income Method**. I was sticking to the teacher lane of the Messenger Product Map. First came the mini offer, the mini-course that got my foot in the door. Then came the main offer, the flagship course that went deeper. And eventually, the max offer—a full-blown membership site with coaching and community.

This chapter is about how you can do the same. Whether you're a writer, a teacher, a speaker, or a coach, there's power in picking one lane and sticking with it. Instead of feeling overwhelmed by all the things you *could* do, you'll stay focused, build depth, and scale your income in a way that's sustainable. Welcome to the **Single Lane Income Method**—your blueprint for scaling by doing less but doing it better.

Why Some Struggle to Scale

Many entrepreneurs feel pressure to juggle writing, teaching, speaking, and coaching. They think they must tap every income stream to succeed. This can seem like the best way to cover all the bases and maximize opportunities. So, they launch a book, then start a course, while offering coaching on the side, all while trying to book speaking gigs.

It's a lot. And for some, it works. But for many, this approach leads to scattered energy and a sense of constant hustle without meaningful progress. Their work feels disconnected, and their results are inconsistent. Instead of scaling smoothly, they find themselves spread thin and struggling to gain real traction in any one area.

When Focusing on One Lane is the Smart Move

There's a time to branch out, but often, sticking to one lane at first can give you the stability and momentum you need to scale. This isn't about limiting your options forever. It's about building a solid foundation in one area before expanding into others.

When you focus on one lane—whether that's writing, teaching, speaking, or coaching—you give yourself the space to master that role. You're not bouncing between different skill sets, trying to be everything to everyone. Instead, you get to go deep, hone your craft, and develop a clear path to scale. It's like choosing to master one sport instead of playing four different ones.

Once you've built authority and expertise in one lane, expanding into others becomes much easier—and more sustainable. You've got the systems, the audience, and the confidence to explore new avenues without feeling overwhelmed.

Finding Balance Between Lanes

This approach doesn't mean you'll never jump between roles. In fact, many entrepreneurs eventually expand across all four influencer voices. But it's important to recognize when you're ready to take on more and when staying focused is the best way to grow. By sticking to one lane first, you can build depth before stretching yourself too thin.

If you're spinning your wheels or jumping between projects, it may be time to focus on just one for now.

The Single Lane Income Method

Remember, the goal here is to focus on one skill set (writer, teacher, speaker, or coach) and create multiple income streams. Let's walk through the steps together.

Step 1: Identify Your Influencer Voice

Before you dive into scaling, the first thing you need to do is figure out which role (or skill set) comes most naturally to you. Are you a writer, teacher, speaker, or coach at heart? This is about understanding where you truly shine and where your strengths align with your passion. When you're doing work that feels like second nature, the process becomes smoother, and the results speak for themselves.

Think back to the times when you felt most energized by your work. Was it when you were writing a book or blog post? Maybe teaching a course or giving a talk lit you up. Or perhaps coaching someone through a problem gave you that sense of purpose. This reflection is key to understanding which lane to stick with for now.

It's like choosing a road on a cross-country journey. If you keep switching routes, you'll lose your way. But if you stay in one lane, you can focus on the ride, get to know the landscape, and actually enjoy the journey. That clarity helps you go further, faster, without feeling overwhelmed.

If you still feel stuck on choosing one lane (writer, teacher, speaker, or coach), then take a look at the product offers in the Messenger Product Map. Are there offers in one of the lanes that you are the most excited about creating? For example, under the writer category, you have low-content books, compact books, and book series. If that is more exciting to you, then some of the other offers in other categories, go with that.

	Mini	Main	Max
Writer	Low-Content Book	Compact Book	Book Series
Teacher	Mini-Course	Flagship Course	Membership Site
Speaker	Paid Virtual Workshop	Paid Speaking Gigs	Host In-Person Events
Coach	4-Week Group Coaching	1-on-1 Coaching	Coaching Membership

Step 2: Start with a Mini Offer

After you've figured out your lane, it's time to get something out into the world. Don't overthink it. Your first step should be a mini offer—a simple, easy-to-launch product that lets you validate your idea. This isn't about perfection; it's about getting real feedback and testing the waters.

Start small. Whether you're a writer, teacher, speaker, or coach, there's always a quick way to create something valuable without spending months on it.

Here are some examples of what a mini offer could look like in your lane:

- **Writer Mini Offer**: A low-content book (like a guided journal or workbook). This allows you to get your feet wet with publishing and see how your audience responds.

- **Teacher Mini Offer**: A mini-course with 7 to 12 short lessons. Focus on one specific problem your audience faces and offer a simple solution.

- **Speaker Mini Offer**: A paid virtual workshop. This could be a 1-2 hour Zoom session where you share valuable insights and engage with your audience.

- **Coach Mini Offer**: A 4-week group coaching program. Keep it small, intimate, and focused on helping your participants achieve a specific outcome.

Remember, "Done is better than perfect." Don't get caught up in making it flawless. The goal is to launch something and gather real-world feedback.

Step 3: Progress to a Main Offer

Once your mini offer has gained traction, it's time to build upon that success. Your audience has shown interest, and they're ready for more. This is where you create your main offer—a deeper, more comprehensive product that provides even more value.

Think of it like adding a second story to your house. The foundation is solid, and now you're expanding to create more space for growth.

Here's what a main offer could look like for each lane:

- **Writer Main Offer**: A compact book. This is a step up from the low-content book but still manageable. It's usually half as long as a traditional book. This lets you publish quickly while providing deeper insights.

- **Teacher Main Offer**: A flagship course. This is your deep dive, typically 15 to 30 lessons, covering a broader topic and offering a complete transformation for your students.

- **Speaker Main Offer**: Paid speaking gigs. Now that you've run virtual workshops, it's time to offer yourself for live events, either in-person or virtual. You can create a speaker page showcasing your talks and give event planners a clear path to hire you.

- **Coach Main Offer**: 1-on-1 coaching. Now that you've run group programs, some people will want more personalized attention. Offer tailored coaching packages that let you work closely with clients to achieve their goals.

This stage is about delivering more depth and value to your audience, and it allows you to increase your prices. Your audience already trusts you, and they're ready to invest in the next step.

Step 4: Scale to the Max Offer

With your main offer thriving, the final step is to scale up to a Max Offer. Here, you elevate your business. Create a product or system that provides ongoing value and generates recurring income.

Your max offer should provide long-term engagement and high impact. Here's what it could look like in each lane:

- **Writer Max Offer**: A book series. Writing one book is great, but a series keeps readers coming back for more. It builds your authority and keeps your audience engaged over time.

- **Teacher Max Offer**: A membership site. This allows you to provide ongoing education with a mix of evergreen content and monthly updates. Your students pay a recurring fee to access exclusive content and resources.

- **Speaker Max Offer**: Hosting in-person events. This could be your own conference or workshop where you gather a community around your message. It's an opportunity to deepen relationships and offer more immersive experiences.

- **Coach Max Offer**: A coaching membership. Here, your clients get ongoing access to group coaching calls, resources, and a community of peers. It's different from a standard membership site because your personal involvement in coaching is what drives its value.

This is where the long-term revenue comes in. You want a system that runs well and adds value. It should help you scale your income and impact without launching new products.

As the saying goes, "Don't limit your challenges; challenge your limits." By scaling to a Max Offer, you challenge yourself. You must create something that goes beyond one-time offers. It must build a sustainable business model.

Today's Exercise: Create Your Single Lane Income Map

Now that you've learned about the Single Lane Income Method and how to scale from a mini offer to a max offer, it's time to put these concepts into action. These steps will help you find your lane and build your offers. They are practical and manageable.

1. **Identify Your Lane**

   ○ Take 10-15 minutes to reflect on your strengths. Are you naturally drawn to writing, teaching, speaking, or coaching? Think about your past experiences and where you've seen the most success or felt the most energized.

○ Write down a brief description of your influencer voice. It could be as simple as, "I'm a teacher because I love explaining complex ideas in simple ways." Or, "I'm a coach because I get energy from helping others achieve their goals."

○ Make sure to stay honest with yourself. If you try to force yourself into a lane that doesn't align with your strengths, scaling will be more difficult down the road.

2. **Brainstorm Your Mini Offer**

○ Based on your chosen lane, list three possible Mini Offers you could create. Think of something that can be completed quickly (in a matter of weeks, not months) and tested with your audience.

- **Example for Writers**: A short ebook or workbook.

- **Example for Teachers**: A mini-course on a specific topic.

- **Example for Speakers**: A 1-2 hour paid virtual workshop.

- **Example for Coaches**: A 4-week group coaching program.

○ Choose one idea that feels the most feasible to complete and will provide value to your audience.

3. **Plan Your Main Offer**

○ Now, think about what your main offer would be. Write down how you could build upon your mini offer to create a more in-depth product that offers greater value. Consider what your audience will want next after experiencing your Mini Offer.

- **Example for Writers**: A compact book or a more comprehensive ebook series.

- **Example for Teachers**: A flagship course that expands on your mini-course with more modules and deeper content.

- **Example for Speakers**: Paid speaking engagements or a larger-scale virtual event.

- **Example for Coaches**: One-on-one coaching or a longer, more intensive group program.

4. Envision Your Max Offer

○ Lastly, start imagining what your Max Offer could look like. This is your long-term plan, where you'll scale your business to create recurring revenue. Write down your ideas for a Max Offer, keeping in mind the examples provided earlier.

- **Example for Writers**: A full book series with multiple installments.

- **Example for Teachers**: A membership site with ongoing courses and resources.

- **Example for Speakers**: Hosting in-person events or a signature annual conference.

- **Example for Coaches**: A coaching membership with regular group calls and community access.

- Map out the steps you need to take to move from your mini offer to your Main Offer and, finally, to your Max Offer. This plan doesn't need to be perfect—just a roadmap that helps guide you as you grow.

5. **Take Action**

- Pick one action you can take this week to start moving forward. Whether it's outlining your mini offer, drafting content for your main offer, or sketching out the structure of your max offer, the key is to start. The first step is always the hardest, but once you get the ball rolling, momentum will follow.

This exercise will help you get clarity on your lane and start laying the groundwork for scaling your income. The key is to start small, validate your ideas, and then gradually build bigger offers as you gain confidence and feedback from your audience.

Key Takeaways:

- Focusing on one lane—writing, teaching, speaking, or coaching—builds depth and expertise. It creates a solid foundation for scaling your income.

- Start with a simple mini offer to test your ideas. Get feedback. Then, expand to a main offer and, eventually, a max offer for recurring revenue.

- Staying in your lane prevents overwhelm. It enables sustainable growth. You can then master your craft and build a scalable, long-term business.

9

Your Income Stream Compass

I magine you're standing in the middle of a vast landscape with endless paths stretching in all directions. There's no single way forward. Instead, you're holding a compass that points toward various destinations, each with its own promise of opportunity and growth. Some paths are clear and straightforward, while others twist and turn, hinting at a slower journey but possibly a more rewarding one. This compass isn't directing you down a pre-determined route. Instead, it guides you toward options, letting you choose the direction that feels right based on where you are now and what you want to accomplish.

Imagine that the compass represents your unique strengths, resources, and goals. It's a tool, not a map. Rather than following a rigid path or jumping into an income stream that "worked for someone else," you're encouraged to decide what feels most achievable and worthwhile. Each income stream you consider has its own benefits and challenges. Some may require more time, some a certain skill set, and others might call for a deeper connection with your audience. But this chapter isn't about taking just any path—it's about choosing the one that fits you best right now. This isn't about being led; it's about feeling empowered to explore.

The purpose here is simple: to help you select an income stream aligned with your abilities, resources, and where you are in your journey. In the rest of this book, you'll learn to create the twelve income streams from the Messenger Product Map. These chapters are not designed to be read straight through (although you can). I want to give you permission to jump ahead to the income stream you are most excited to create first.

This is a personalized journey. No two people will need the same approach, and that's the beauty of it. The journey isn't linear; it's personal. This chapter will help you choose wisely and with confidence. It will set you up to scale your income in an exciting, achievable way.

Steer Clear of the Hustle Trap: Find the Path That's Right for You

Most people start out eager and ready to dive in, but they lack a clear direction. They look to others for ideas, grabbing onto income streams that seem successful for someone else, hoping they'll see the same results. Maybe they hear about someone who made it big with online courses, so they decide to jump into creating one, too. Or they see a coach thriving with one-on-one sessions and think, "That's what I need to do." But here's the catch: what works for one person doesn't necessarily work for another.

Choosing a path just because it helped someone else is risky. It may lead you to a project that doesn't suit your strengths or situation. You might take on a high-effort project. It may need hours you don't have. Or, you might need a skill you don't yet have. Without knowing your own resources, you will be frustrated. These include your time, energy, and unique skills. The result? Burnout. Confusion. Progress that barely inches forward. Instead of building momentum, you end up feeling drained, wondering why it's not working out the way you'd hoped. The problem isn't lack of effort; it's misaligned effort.

To move forward with purpose, start by looking inward. Imagine that internal compass guiding you rather than just jumping on whatever seems popular. Begin with a simple assessment of where you stand—your interests, time, resources, and skills. Each point on this compass aligns with a different income stream. It offers a path that feels realistic, manageable, and meaningful to you. The goal is to match your direction to what's achievable right now. Using this internal compass, you're not just picking an income stream. You're choosing a route that feels like yours, built on a solid, sustainable foundation.

Identify Your Strengths

Starting with what you're naturally good at isn't just wise—it's necessary. Writing, speaking, coaching, and teaching are more than skills. They are pathways that tap into your strengths and interests. By leveraging what already feels natural, you give yourself a head start. For example, if you're someone who feels energized when connecting one-on-one, then coaching may be a natural fit. Or if you're a born writer who finds flow in creating content, maybe an ebook or blog series is the perfect entry point. When you build from your strengths, you're not just working hard; you're working smart, aligning effort with ease.

Understand Your Audience's Needs

Success in any income stream is deeply rooted in knowing what your audience actually wants. Too often, creators jump into a new offer based on their own interests, only to discover it doesn't resonate with the people they're trying to reach. Think of it as a two-way street: your skills and interests meet your audience's needs. If you're a skilled teacher, consider your audience. Do they want short, actionable lessons? Or do they prefer in-depth, multi-part courses? The more your offer aligns with what your audience is already looking for, the easier it is to gain traction and build lasting connections.

Consult the Messenger Product Map

The Messenger Product Map lays out twelve income streams across four core lanes: writer, teacher, speaker, and coach. This map offers a framework to help you narrow your focus, guiding you toward a lane that suits your strengths.

	Mini	Main	Max
Writer	Low-Content Book	Compact Book	Book Series
Teacher	Mini-Course	Flagship Course	Membership Site
Speaker	Paid Virtual Workshop	Paid Speaking Gigs	Host In-Person Events
Coach	4-Week Group Coaching	1-on-1 Coaching	Coaching Membership

After choosing a lane, consider the scale of your offer: mini, main, or max. Mini offers can be a low-commitment start, ideal if you're short on time or resources. Main offers are deeper and need a moderate investment. Max offers create a high-impact, often high-ticket experience. Your choice depends on your resources and stage of business. Each option is a stepping stone, providing a manageable way to move forward in a focused direction.

Balance Quick Wins and Long-Term Investments

Not all income streams provide instant results, and that's okay. In fact, balancing quick wins with long-term investments is key to creating sustainable momentum. A quick win, like a low-content book, can boost your confidence. A long-term investment, like a membership site, takes time to build. But it can yield steady, recurring income. By choosing a mix, you allow yourself to see short-term rewards without sacrificing your long-term growth. It's like planting a garden with fast-growing herbs and slow-growing trees; each has its place and purpose, nourishing you in different ways.

Avoid Analysis Paralysis

There's no perfect choice, and waiting for one only holds you back. Each income stream brings its own set of advantages, but none are flawless. Instead of getting stuck in endless comparisons, focus on what makes the most sense for you right now. Maybe you don't have all the time in the world, so a mini-offer is best. Or perhaps you're ready to commit to something more substantial. The key is to take a step forward, knowing you can always refine and pivot. Making a choice doesn't lock you in forever—it simply sets you on a path. And sometimes, the best way to see the path clearly is just to start walking.

Today's Exercise: Map Out Your Income Stream Path

Let's get practical. You're holding the compass; now it's time to use it. Think of this exercise as creating your personal map. Your journey will be unique, and your next step should feel purposeful based on what you're ready to do right now. Remember, you don't have to follow the rest of the book in order. Feel free to jump ahead and locate the chapter that covers the income stream you're most excited to create next.

Here's how to get started:

- **List Your Strengths and Skills**: Grab a pen and take a moment to jot down what you're good at. Are you a natural speaker? Do you love writing? Maybe you're great at connecting with people one-on-one. Knowing your strengths gives you a strong base to build on. It beats starting with something that might feel forced.

- **Assess Your Resources**: Next, write down what you have available right now in terms of time, budget, and tools. Do you have an hour a day to dedicate, or just a couple of hours each week? Knowing your resources will help you choose an income stream that's realistic for your life as it is now, not as you hope it might be someday.

- **Identify Your Audience's Needs**: Take a step back and reflect on what your audience craves most from you. What questions do they frequently ask? What content do they respond to? These insights will help you align your offer with something your audience is already hungry for.

- **Select Your Top Income Streams**: Now, take a look at the Messenger Product Map. Circle the income streams that align with your strengths, resources, and audience needs. Which options stand out? Focus on the ones that meet all three areas, giving you the best chance of creating something valuable and doable.

- **Choose One to Pursue**: Finally, commit to a single income stream to explore next. This doesn't mean you're stuck with it forever; it's simply a starting point. Dive into the chapter that covers your chosen income stream and begin making it a reality.

This exercise isn't about making a perfect choice—it's about making the next right move. By mapping out your path, you'll have a clearer sense of direction, confidence in your next steps, and a plan rooted in your unique strengths.

Key Takeaways:

- Your internal compass guides you. It is your strengths, resources, and audience needs. It leads you to the best income stream for your current journey.

- Skip around this book freely, focusing on the income streams that resonate most; this isn't a linear path but a flexible roadmap.

- Start with one income stream that aligns with you and commit to exploring it, knowing you can refine or change direction as you grow.

10

The Writer's Mini Offer: A Low-Content Book

B ack in 2008, Angela Mader was just like many of us - frustrated with the available options for tracking her fitness journey. So what did she do? She created her own journal. Little did she know, this personal project would spark a revolution in the fitness industry.

Mader's Fitbook wasn't just another pretty notebook. It was a 12-week fitness tracker designed with purpose. Compact, comprehensive, and motivational - it filled a gap in the market that no one else had noticed.

Here's the kicker: Mader didn't spend years perfecting her product. She took action. With a small initial print run, she launched the Fitbook in late 2008. Within a year, Mader's humble journal caught the eye of major retailers. Walgreens and Sports Authority? They wanted in.

The Fitbook flew off shelves.[4] Why? It solved a real problem for real people. It wasn't just a product; it was a fitness companion. Success breeds success. The original Fitbook paved the way for an entire product line:

• Fitbook Lite

• Fitbook Junior

• Fitbook Mama

Each version catered to a specific audience, proving that niches matter. By 2012, Mader's company, Fitlosophy, was raking in over $1.5 million in annual sales. But Mader didn't stop there. She embraced the digital age, launching apps and online tools to complement her physical journals.

Now, you might be thinking, "That's great for Mader, but what does it mean for me?"

Here's the golden nugget: Mader's success hinged on a low-content book. There were no dense chapters, no complex theories, just simple, useful pages designed to help people track their progress.

This is the power of low-content books. They're quick to produce, easy to use, and can solve real-world problems. They're the secret weapon in your writing arsenal. The low-content book world is ripe with opportunity. It's not about writing the next great novel. It's about creating tools that make people's lives better.

The Allure of the Traditional Book

You've got a brilliant idea for a book. It's going to change lives, maybe even the world. You dive in headfirst, pouring your heart and soul onto the pages. Months fly by. Maybe even years. You're crafting every sentence with care, polishing every chapter to perfection.

Sound familiar?

This is the path many aspiring authors take. They focus all their energy on creating a masterpiece – a full-length, text-heavy book that'll knock the socks off readers. It's admirable, sure. But is it smart?

Here's the kicker: While you're busy writing away in isolation, the market is moving. Trends are shifting. Reader preferences are evolving. And you? You're in the dark.

The Pitfalls of the Traditional Approach

Let's break it down:

- Time Sink: You're investing months, maybe years, into a project without any real-world feedback.

- Market Mystery: You have no clue if there's actually a demand for your book. It's a shot in the dark.

- Missed Opportunities: While you're heads down on your magnum opus, you could be missing out on quick wins and valuable market insights.

Think about it. What if you spend two years writing a book on productivity hacks for busy parents, only to find out that your target audience is more interested in quick, actionable tips they can implement on the go?

Or worse, what if the market is saturated with similar books by the time you're ready to publish?

It's like baking a massive, elaborate cake without knowing if anyone at the party likes that flavor. You might end up with a beautiful creation that nobody wants to eat.

The Risk Factor

Here's the harsh truth: This approach is a high-stakes gamble. You're betting all your chips on one big play. If it hits, great. But if it misses? That's a lot of time, effort, and potentially money down the drain.

And let's not forget the emotional toll. Imagine pouring your heart into a book for years, only to have it flop on launch day. Ouch.

So, what's the alternative? How can you test the waters before diving in headfirst? Well, that's where our mini offer comes in. But more on that in a bit. First, let's talk about why this shift in approach could be a game-changer for your writing career.

A Smarter Way to Write

Ever heard the phrase "work smarter, not harder"? Well, it's time to apply that to your writing career. Let's flip the script on the traditional publishing approach.

Enter: Low-Content Books

Imagine creating a book in days, not months. A book that could start earning you money and valuable insights almost immediately. Sounds too good to be true? It's not. Welcome to the world of low-content books.

These aren't your typical novels or non-fiction tomes. We're talking journals, planners, and workbooks - books that are light on text but heavy on utility. And they're your secret weapon for kickstarting your writing career.

Your Market Research Superpower

Think of low-content books as your crystal ball. They give you a sneak peek into what your audience wants. How? By putting a real product into their hands, fast.

You're not just guessing what people might like. You're giving them something tangible and seeing how they respond. It's like a taste test for your ideas.

Did your gratitude journal fly off the shelves? Boom – you've just discovered a hungry market. Did your workout planner barely get a glance? That's valuable info, too. You've saved yourself from investing months in a full-length fitness book that might have flopped.

Speed is Your Friend

In the world of publishing, speed can be a game-changer. With low-content books, you can go from idea to published product in record time. Why does this matter?

• Quick Feedback: The faster you publish, the faster you learn. Each book becomes a mini-experiment, providing real-world data on what works and what doesn't.

• Rapid Income: Why wait years for your first author paycheck? Start earning sooner and reinvest in your writing career.

• Market Agility: Spot a trend? You can have a relevant product out while it's still hot. Try doing that with a traditional book!

The Snowball Effect

Here's where it gets really exciting. Each low-content book you create builds on the last. You're not just making products. You're building a brand, growing an audience, and gaining insights with every release.

And the best part? All of this is laying the groundwork for your bigger projects. By the time you're ready to write that full-length book, you'll have a clear picture of what your audience wants and a platform to launch from.

Ready to dive in? Let's explore how to make this work for you.

Crafting Your Low-Content Book: A Step-by-Step Guide

Define Your Book's Purpose and Audience

Start by identifying the type of low-content book you want to create. Will it be a workbook, journal, planner, or a hybrid? Consider your target audience and their specific needs. What challenges do they face? What goals are they trying to achieve?

Brainstorm at least five topic ideas that align with your expertise and your audience's interests. The more focused your concept, the more valuable your book will be. Remember, clarity at this stage sets the foundation for a successful project.

Design Your Book Template

Using a tool like Canva or another design platform, create a template for your book. Include all the essential elements:

- An eye-catching cover

- A welcoming first page

- Copyright notice

- Table of contents

Customize your design with fonts, colors, and graphics that reflect your brand. Keep in mind that good design isn't just about aesthetics—it's about functionality. Your book should be visually appealing and easy to use.

Develop Your Content Pages

Create master layouts for your core content pages. This could include daily journal prompts, workbook exercises, or planner layouts. Aim for a clean, inviting design that's easy to replicate throughout the book.

Keep your color palette minimal. This not only creates a cohesive look but also helps keep printing costs down if you decide to offer a physical version of your book.

Generate Valuable Content

This is where you'll create the meat of your book. Write prompts, summaries, exercises, or reflections that provide real value to your readers. Consider using AI tools to help generate ideas, but always review and edit the content to ensure it aligns with your voice and brand.

Focus on creating content that's clear, concise, and relevant to your audience's needs. Ask yourself: What questions do my readers have? What insights or inspiration do they need? How can I help them reach their goals?

Refine and Polish

Before finalizing your book, take the time to review and refine every page. Check for typos, formatting issues, and overall clarity. Ensure that all pages are in the correct order and that the book flows logically from start to finish.

Consider asking a friend or professional to proofread your work. A fresh pair of eyes can often catch errors or inconsistencies you might have missed.

Remember, creating a low-content book is about providing value in a concise, accessible format. By following these steps, you can create a resource that resonates with your audience and supports your business goals. Focus on your readers' needs.

Your low-content book has the potential to be a powerful tool for your audience and a valuable asset for your business. With careful planning, design, and content, you can create a book that stands out and serves your readers.

Today's Exercise: Your Low-Content Book Idea Generator

Let's create a simple, pressure-free exercise to help you come up with your low-content book idea and type.

Step 1: Passion Points

List 3 to 5 topics you're passionate about or have significant experience in. These could be hobbies, professional skills, or life experiences.

Step 2: Problem Spotting

For each topic you listed, think of a common problem or challenge people face. Write these down next to your topics.

Step 3: Book Type Matching

Now, consider which type of low-content book might best address each problem:

• Journal: for reflection or tracking

• Workbook: for learning or skill development

• Planner: for organization and goal-setting

• Combo: a mix of the above

Jot down the book type(s) that seem most suitable next to each problem.

Step 4: Choose Your Favorite

Review your list. Which combination of topic, problem, and book type resonates with you most? Circle or highlight it.

Step 5: Quick Concept Sketch

For your chosen idea, briefly answer these questions:

• Who would be most interested in this book?

• What's one unique feature your book could have?

• If you had to give it a title right now, what might it be?

Congratulations! You've just generated a solid concept for your low-content book. You've found a topic you're passionate about. It can solve a problem. You've chosen the best type of book for it. You've identified your target audience. You have a unique feature and a potential title.

This exercise will match your knowledge and interests with books that can serve your audience. Remember, this is just the starting point. Feel free to refine and evolve your idea as you move forward with creating your low-content book.

Key Takeaways:

• Low-content books are a quick way to test demand and make money. They are a perfect Writer Mini Offer for aspiring authors and entrepreneurs.

• By quickly creating and publishing, you can get feedback. This will validate your ideas before you invest time in larger projects. It reduces risk and boosts your chances of success.

- The Writer Mini Offer strategy lets you scale your income. Create multiple low-content books, build a brand, and test the market. You may then transition to full-length books or other products.

11

The Writer's Main Offer: A Compact Book

In January 2012, I had a stubborn goal that I couldn't shake: write a book. It stared back at me every year, untouched. Although publishing on Amazon was still new, it was possible. The problem was that I had no experience writing a book and didn't know how to get one published.

I thought, "What if I approached writing a book like writing blog posts?" I'd been comfortable writing 1,000-word blog posts for the past two years. What if I didn't need to write a full-length book? What if a shorter book could work?

So, I made a plan. I'd write the equivalent of one blog post per day for 20 days, then use the last 10 days to edit and publish. I didn't overthink it; I just started. Thirty days later, my first book was published.

That 20,000-word Kindle book was far from traditional. It was short, but it got traction. Enough traction that a college professor reached out to me and made my compact book required reading for his freshman class.

You don't have to write a 60,000-word epic to make an impact. A shorter book can do the job. This chapter is about why writing a compact book—half the size of a regular one—could be the smartest move you can make.

Why overwhelm yourself when you don't have to? Let's dive into why less can be more.

Chasing the Myth of the "Big Book"

Most aspiring authors picture their first book as a hefty 60,000-word epic. It's what they've seen on the shelves, so it feels like the only way to be taken seriously. They dive into the process with big dreams of writing a book that feels substantial, impressive, or even monumental.

But reality hits hard. What starts as excitement quickly turns into stress. The word count seems like a mountain they can't scale. Writers find themselves staring at a blank page, overwhelmed by the enormity of the task in front of them. A project that could have been simple becomes a mental roadblock, stretching over months or even years. And the worst part? Many never finish.

So why do so many of us fall into this trap? We've been taught to believe that more words equal more credibility. To be respected, we have to write something *big*. But here's the truth: the size of your book doesn't determine its value. Your message does.

Drowning in Word Count

A long book sounds good in theory, but the reality is different. The bigger the word count, the bigger the pressure. Every chapter feels like another brick being stacked on top of you. The deeper you get into it, the heavier it feels.

Writing a book this long doesn't just take more time—it drains your energy. Each week that passes, you lose momentum. What started as a passion becomes a grind. A task that should feel fulfilling now feels like work you can't finish.

At some point, many give up. They put the book on the shelf (figuratively, because it's nowhere near finished), and it collects dust. Months, sometimes years, go by, and that book—the one they dreamed of—never sees the light of day.

The Problem with "Filler"

When the goal is to hit a certain word count, authors often end up filling their books with extra content. Tangents, unnecessary details, and repetitive ideas sneak in. The book starts to drift from the original message.

Instead of delivering something concise and powerful, the book loses its focus. The reader senses it, too. They start skimming pages, looking for the meat, but they have to wade through filler to get there. What could have been a punchy, impactful read turns into a slog.

Longer doesn't always mean better. More pages don't equal more impact. In fact, stretching your book just to hit a target can make it *less* impactful.

The Case for a Compact Book

Instead of chasing that 60,000-word finish line, consider taking a different approach. A compact book—half the length but packed with value. It's not about cutting corners; it's about focusing on what really matters. When you strip away the fluff, you're left with something lean and powerful.

A compact book is quicker to write, faster to edit, and easier to publish. Instead of spending months, even years, wrestling with your manuscript, you can get your ideas out there in a fraction of the time. The sooner your book is in readers' hands, the sooner it can start making an impact.

Clarity is the goal. When you write a compact book, you're forced to make every word count. There's no room for meandering or unnecessary details. You dive straight into the heart of your message and stay there. Readers appreciate this. In a world full of distractions, they're looking for something that gets to the point without wasting their time.

And that's the beauty of a compact book: it respects the reader's time. It offers them something they can digest in one or two sittings. They walk away feeling satisfied, not overwhelmed, because you've delivered exactly what they needed—no more, no less.

This is what makes compact books so powerful. You're giving your readers a faster path to the insight they're looking for. Less is more.

Why a Compact Book Works

Speed to Market

When you're writing a compact book, you're not bogged down by endless chapters or sprawling narratives. You get to the point faster, which means your book gets out there faster. The moment your book hits the market, it starts doing the work for you. Readers get their hands on your ideas sooner, and that momentum starts building. Instead of waiting months or even years to publish, you can go from idea to finished product in a fraction of the time. The faster you release, the faster you can connect with your audience, drive engagement, and see real results.

Laser-Focused Content

Compact books don't leave room for fluff. They force you to cut straight to the core of your message. This sharpens your writing and ensures that every page delivers something valuable. Readers feel that focus. They don't get lost in long-winded explanations or off-topic tangents. Instead, they get actionable insights that stick. When you distill your message into its most essential form, you amplify its impact. It's like hitting them with the heart of the message right from the start, with no distractions along the way.

Easier Production

Writing a book is a big project. But when you cut down the word count, you cut down the workload. A compact book is faster to write, easier to edit, and quicker to publish. The whole process feels more manageable. Instead of staring down a seemingly endless to-do list, you're looking at something you can wrap up efficiently. This lowers the chances of hitting that "abandoned project" point. A shorter, more achievable goal keeps you moving forward without getting bogged down.

Readers Want Shorter Books

Today's readers are busy. They're looking for something they can consume quickly and still feel like they've gained value. A compact book delivers that experience. It respects their time and attention. Readers love something they can pick up, finish in a few sittings, and immediately apply what they've learned. In a world of distractions, your book is the answer. It's a quick, insightful read that won't waste their time.

Lower Barrier to Entry

The idea of writing a full-length book can be intimidating, especially if it's your first time. A compact book changes that. The shorter format feels less overwhelming and less impossible. It opens the door for first-time authors who want to get a taste of the self-publishing process without feeling crushed by a huge project. It's like dipping your toes in the water rather than diving straight into the deep end.

Faster Return on Investment

A compact book doesn't just save you time; it helps you start earning sooner. You get your product out to the market quickly, which means you can start seeing returns faster. The sooner your book is available, the better. It will boost book sales, grow your audience, and generate business leads. You can then test your ideas, make money, and build credibility. It's not just about writing—it's about putting your business in motion.

Today's Exercise: Map Out Your Compact Book Writing Plan

Instead of just following the writing process, let's map out a clear, personalized plan for your compact book. Here's how to break it down:

1. **Choose Your Core Message**

   ○ Pick a single focused idea that you're passionate about and can fully cover in a compact format (15,000-30,000 words).

- Think of it as solving a problem or providing a specific solution for your readers.

2. Identify Your Audience

- Who are you writing this book for? Be as specific as possible. Understand their needs, challenges, and what they hope to gain from your book.

3. Mind Map Your Idea

- Set aside 10 minutes to brainstorm everything you know about your topic. Write down all your ideas, insights, and subtopics that could support your main message.

4. Organize Your Chapters

- Turn your mind map into 5 to 7 key chapters. Each chapter should focus on one major idea that pushes your reader closer to the solution you're offering.

5. Create a Writing Schedule

- Aim to write 1,000 words per day, which will result in a 20,000-word book in 20 days. Stick to one chapter at a time to stay focused.

6. Plan Your Editing Time

- Set aside 10 days after you finish writing to edit and polish your book.

- Focus on simplifying, removing fluff, and improving clarity.

7. **Outline Your Publishing Strategy**

- How will you format your book (Kindle, paperback, etc.)?

- Create a checklist for preparing your book cover, formatting, and uploading to Amazon or other platforms.

8. **Set a Deadline**

- Choose a deadline for publishing your book.

- This will keep you accountable and motivated to follow through.

By mapping out these steps, you'll have a clear, manageable plan to write and publish your compact book efficiently. The key is to stay focused, work on it daily, and avoid overcomplicating the process. Ready to get started?

Key Takeaways:

- A compact book gets your message out faster and with more focus. It helps you connect with readers, without the overwhelm of writing a traditional book.

- By focusing on clarity and cutting out filler, a shorter book delivers more value in less time, which resonates with today's busy readers.

- A compact book is easier for new authors to write. It lets you test your ideas in the market quickly and earn a faster return on your efforts.

12

The Writer's Max Offer: A Book Series

E very year, I take a 30-day sabbatical in July. It's a break from the day-to-day grind, but more than that, it's a chance to step back and get a bird's-eye view of my business. After running an online business since 2009, I've learned that you have to pause, look at the bigger picture, and figure out what's next. It's a chance to see where the business needs to pivot and evolve.

In July 2023, I walked away from my sabbatical with a theme: peaceful systems and peaceful profits. I wanted to simplify things. I needed a fresh purpose, a new vision that went beyond just providing for my family or doing what I love. Those things are great, but after doing this for so long, I wanted something more.

It all started with a whiteboard. I asked myself one question: "What things actually leave a legacy?" I needed to brainstorm how my life and work could make an impact beyond my time here. The list came quickly.

- Writing and publishing books.

- Starting a non-profit.

- Equipping others to make an impact.

- Leaving an inheritance.

- Starting a church.

But one thing stood out immediately—*writing and publishing books.*

I love online courses, memberships, coaching programs, and work-shops, but books leave a legacy. I thought about the authors who have shaped me, and most of them aren't even alive anymore. Yet, their words still have power. Books like *Acres of Diamonds* by Russell Conwell, *7 Habits of Highly Effective People* by Stephen Covey, *How to Win Friends and Influence People* by Dale Carnegie, *Mere Christianity* by C.S. Lewis, and so many others. Their words continue to make an impact long after they're gone.

That's when it hit me. I could combine this idea of peaceful systems and peaceful profits by creating a book series. By putting multiple books on Amazon, I could create recurring income from royalties. These books could grow my email list. From there, I could guide readers to my membership sites and then to my coaching member-ships.

Today, I'm a little over a year into this strategy. As I write this, you're holding the fifth book in my series.

The One-Book Myth

Most writers fall into the trap of thinking that one book can change everything. They focus all their energy on a single manuscript. They spend months—sometimes years—polishing every word, every chapter. They dream of their book hitting bestseller lists, imagining that success will follow naturally from there. This mindset often leads to a fixation on perfection, where every small detail must be just right before they can release the book to the world.

Traditional publishing has fueled this idea for years. Writers believe that only a book deal can bring long-term success. They think they must work with a publisher and write long, exhaustive manuscripts.

A lot of time is spent waiting. Waiting for acceptance, for edits, and for the right moment to launch. The entire journey from manuscript to finished product can stretch on for years.

But what's the reality? Most authors don't see the success they envisioned. They're left with a single book that may—or may not—gain traction in the market. Meanwhile, they've invested an incredible amount of time and energy into something that might not deliver the results they hoped for.

The Perfectionism Trap

Perfectionism is the silent enemy of progress. When you spend years trying to perfect one book, you miss out on the bigger picture. Writing one long, perfect book sounds great in theory, but it drastically limits your potential. Why? Because the world moves fast, and so do your readers. Readers' tastes shift, market trends change, and new books are published every day. As you perfect every sentence, other authors are publishing new work and growing their readership.

In the meantime, focusing on a single book leaves you vulnerable. A shift in the market or an unexpected event can reduce your book's appeal, and you're left scrambling. Authors who depend on just one book are putting all their eggs in one basket, hoping that one success will sustain them for years. But this narrow focus limits your earning potential. There's only so much money a single book can generate.

Traditional Publishing's Long Road

Traditional publishing doesn't just slow you down—it can cost you creative freedom. When you sign a book deal, you're no longer in control. Decisions about the content, release schedule, and even the cover design are often out of your hands. And the timeline? It's long. It can take years for your book to make it from manuscript to shelf.

In today's fast-paced world, waiting years to release your work leaves you behind. Trends change. Readers' attention shifts. You're not able to adapt quickly, and by the time your book finally hits the shelves, it could already be outdated or irrelevant. The more time that passes, the more disconnected you become from what your audience truly wants.

The Consistent Output Approach

So, what's the alternative? It's not about one perfect book—it's about building a collection. Successful authors understand that consistent output is the key. They focus on creating a steady stream of books, each one targeted to meet specific audience needs. Instead of waiting years to publish, they work on a schedule. They release shorter, impactful books multiple times a year.

This approach doesn't just increase the number of books you have in the market. It multiplies your opportunities for success. Each new book gives readers another entry point to discover your work. Each new release builds momentum, engages your audience, and boosts your chances of creating loyal readers.

Shorter Books, Bigger Impact

Gone are the days when a book had to be 100,000 words to be considered valuable. Today, readers crave concise, actionable content. They want books that they can digest quickly and implement right away. Successful authors know this. They embrace writing shorter books that get straight to the point, cutting out the fluff and focusing on delivering real value.

Not only do shorter books resonate better with readers, but they're also faster to produce. It lets you meet market demands, release content often, and adapt to changes without a multi-year publishing cycle.

Build a Body of Work, Not a One-Hit Wonder

The goal isn't to have just one successful book. The goal is to build a body of work. The more books you have in your catalog, the more opportunities you create for readers to discover you. Every new release boosts the visibility of your entire collection. It's like adding layers to a foundation, each one strengthening the structure.

This strategy isn't about relying on a single hit. It's about multiplying your chances of success by consistently offering new, valuable content. A catalog builds your authority and reach. Every book creates passive income. The more you produce, the more you earn—and the more you learn, allowing you to refine your process and deliver even better content in the future.

Consistency Beats Perfection

Readers don't want to wait years for your next book. They want fresh content regularly. Think about your favorite TV series—when a new season drops, you're excited because you've been following the story. The same applies to your readers. When they see you publishing consistently, they know there's always something new to look forward to.

It's not about writing one perfect book. It's about keeping readers engaged by offering them a steady flow of valuable material. With every book you release, you increase your chances of being discovered by a wider audience. You're not just waiting around for lightning to strike once—you're creating more opportunities for success with every new release. The more books you have out there, the better. Readers may stumble upon one, love your writing, and buy your entire collection.

Leverage Multiple Formats

Don't just stop at a paperback. Today's readers consume books in more ways than ever before. Some prefer to hold a physical book in their hands, while others prefer reading on their Kindle during their commute. And let's not forget about audiobooks—perfect for people who want to listen while they drive, work out, or run errands.

By publishing your books in multiple formats, you're casting a wider net. A single book can reach different types of readers, each with their own preferences. And it doesn't take much extra effort to release your book in these formats. Once your manuscript is done, it's just about making sure it's available everywhere your readers are. More formats equal more readers, which means more royalties in your pocket.

Scale via Shorter Books

The idea that books have to be long to be valuable is outdated. In fact, readers are hungry for shorter, more focused books. They don't have time for fluff—they want quick, actionable insights they can use right away. Shorter books meet that demand.

A focused book that delivers high value in fewer pages resonates more with readers. It feels like they're getting right to the good stuff. And for you, shorter books mean quicker production times. Instead of waiting years to release a huge book, publish several shorter ones each year. This will cater to different niches. You're giving readers exactly what they need while also scaling your output, which leads to more sales, faster.

Repurpose Content

Why reinvent the wheel every time? Content can—and should—be repurposed. Maybe that chapter you wrote for your book would make a great blog post. Or maybe the key points from your latest release could be turned into a workshop or a podcast episode. The beauty of content is that it's flexible.

Repurposing doesn't mean being redundant. It's about reaching your audience in multiple ways, using the same core ideas. Some prefer reading, others listening. Some like interactive workshops. Using the same content on different platforms expands your reach. It also builds a consistent brand across everything you do.

Audience Building Through Volume

A single book can only do so much. But as you publish more books, your presence grows. Volume is a key driver in building an audience. When readers finish one book and see you've written more, they're likely to check out your other titles. Each book becomes an entry point for new readers.

Having a larger catalog also builds credibility. The more you've published, the more serious readers take you. It's like walking into a bakery and seeing shelves full of fresh, delicious pastries—you trust the baker knows what they're doing. The same applies here. With more books under your belt, you're seen as an authority, and that trust translates into sales.

Systemize the Process

Writing a book doesn't have to be chaotic. The key to scaling is creating a system that you can repeat again and again. Templates for book covers, outlines for writing, and checklists for editing can speed up production. They won't sacrifice quality.

By systemizing your approach, you eliminate decision fatigue. You know exactly what needs to be done and when. It's a rinse-and-repeat method that keeps things moving forward. Every time you sit down to write, edit, or design, you're not starting from scratch. You're following a proven process that allows you to focus on what matters most: getting your work out into the world and building your income.

Today's Exercise: Create Your Book Production System

Follow these steps to set up your own streamlined book production process. The goal is to help you consistently publish without feeling overwhelmed.

- **Step 1: Decide on Your Publishing Frequency.** Choose how many books you want to release this year. Start small, like one book every 3 or 4 months. This gives you a clear target.

- **Step 2: Create a Template for Each Step.** Set up templates for your book outline, cover design, and editing process. This will save time every time you start a new project. You can use tools like Canva for covers and Google Docs for outlines.

- **Step 3: Build a Simple Writing Schedule.** Block off specific times each week for writing. Commit to a set number of words per week. This steady output keeps you moving forward.

- **Step 4: Automate the Repetitive Tasks.** Use software to handle repetitive tasks like formatting and editing. Tools like Grammarly, Hemingway, and formatting software can make the process faster.

- **Step 5: Track Your Progress.** Use a simple spreadsheet or checklist to track your progress in writing, editing, and cover design. This helps you see your momentum and stay organized.

By following these steps, you'll create a system. It will let you write books faster and more efficiently. You can then focus on growing your audience and income.

Key Takeaways:

- Writing many books, not just one perfect manuscript is key. It leads to more visibility, credibility, and income.

- Publishing in multiple formats and repurposing content expands your reach. It lets you meet your audience wherever they are.

- Systemizing the book creation process lets you scale your efforts. You can produce more books without sacrificing quality or burning out.

13

The Teacher's Mini Offer: A Mini-Course

B efore *The 4-Hour Workweek* became a bestseller, Tim Ferriss didn't just assume people would buy his book. He wanted to make sure. So, he ran a simple experiment. Ferriss tested different book titles and concepts using small-scale Google Ads. The ads were cheap and quick. Each time someone clicked, Ferriss knew he had struck a chord. This wasn't about selling the book yet—it was about figuring out what people actually cared about.

Ferriss didn't write a full manuscript first. He didn't wait until everything was "perfect." He validated his market with a tiny investment, learned what his audience wanted, and only then did he fully commit. The result? A book that defined a generation of entrepreneurs. And he knew it would sell before he even wrote it.[5]

What does this have to do with you? A mini-course is your Google Ad. It's a way to test the waters. You can see what your audience needs. Then, you can refine your message before spending months on a massive project. Instead of diving headfirst into a full course or program, the mini-course lets you start small, learn fast, and pivot if needed. It's not about having everything figured out—it's about validating your idea first, just like Ferriss did.

That's the power of the mini-course. A simple, focused offer that helps you test your market's interest while refining your content.

Why Most Broad Courses Fall Flat

Most people make the same mistake when they create their first course. They aim for big, broad, and all-encompassing. They try to cover everything they know on a subject, thinking that more information equals more value. So they spend months—sometimes even years—crafting the perfect course. Hours of video content, endless modules, and worksheets designed to cover every possible angle.

Here's the problem: they don't know if anyone actually wants it. They don't know if their course hits the right pain points or solves the most urgent problems. They're guessing, hoping their audience will care. When they finally launch, they're met with silence. Or worse, a handful of students sign up but never make it past the first few lessons.

When you build a course without validating demand first, you're rolling the dice. And the odds aren't in your favor. Here's why:

- **Low sales:** A broad course tries to appeal to everyone, which often means it appeals to no one. It lacks focus, and your audience can't see a clear outcome, so they don't feel motivated to buy.

- **Burnout for you:** You pour your heart into creating something massive, only to discover it doesn't resonate. After all that work, the lack of results can leave you frustrated, drained, and hesitant to try again.

- **Overwhelmed students:** Even when people do sign up, they often feel lost in a sea of information. Too many modules, too much to process—students drop off halfway through, feeling like they'll never reach the end.

The reality? More isn't better. It's just more.

The Smarter Way: Start Small and Validate

The solution is simple: start small. Instead of building an entire course right out of the gate, create a mini-course. Focus on one specific problem and solve it. This approach lets you test the waters without overcommitting.

A mini-course allows you to:

- **Validate demand:** Before you invest months creating content, you can see if people are willing to pay for your expertise.

- **Refine your message:** You'll get real feedback on what resonates, helping you improve and tweak your content.

- **Reduce risk:** With a smaller, more focused course, there's less at stake if you need to pivot or adjust.

Instead of guessing, you're making informed decisions. You're learning what your audience actually needs before diving into something bigger. This not only saves time but builds your confidence as a teacher and course creator.

Steps to Crafting a Successful Mini-Course

Choose a Niche-Specific Topic

One of the biggest mistakes people make is going too broad with their course topic. The broader the course, the harder it is to get anyone's attention. Instead, zoom in on one specific, actionable problem your audience is struggling with. A niche-specific topic is easier to create, market, and sell.

For example, instead of tackling "Healthy Living," narrow it down to "5 Days to Improve Your Gut Health." That's specific, actionable, and much more enticing to someone looking for immediate results.

Think of your mini-course like a spotlight, not a floodlight. It should shine a focused beam on a single problem your audience needs help with. By addressing one clear issue, you'll attract the right people who are eager for a solution.

Frame the Problem and Outcome

People buy transformation, not information. They come to you because they want a change, and your mini-course should promise that change. To do that, you need to clearly frame the problem your audience is facing and the outcome they can expect after completing your course.

What's their "before" state? Frustration? Confusion? Maybe they feel overwhelmed. Now, think about the "after" state. Will they feel confident? Empowered? Relieved?

"People don't buy products, they buy better versions of themselves," says Samuel Hulick. You need to highlight the transformation your mini-course promises. Be specific. Instead of saying, "Learn to manage stress," say, "Reduce your stress in 7 days with simple daily practices." It's all about painting a clear before-and-after picture.

Break It Down into Actionable Steps

Once you've defined the transformation, it's time to create a roadmap to get your students there. Your mini-course should be broken down into bite-sized, actionable steps. Think small, clear, and simple.

Instead of telling your students to "understand gut health," say, "Eliminate processed sugars in Week 1." That's actionable. People know exactly what to do and how to do it.

Teaching a mini-course is like writing a recipe. You're not just listing ingredients; you're walking people through each step until they have a completed dish. Action engages. Information alone overwhelms.

Validate with Feedback

Don't wait until everything's perfect to launch your mini-course. Instead, treat it like a pilot episode. Release it to a small group, gather feedback, and tweak it as needed. You'll learn what resonates and what doesn't before scaling to a larger audience.

As the saying goes, "You can't improve what you don't measure." Early feedback is crucial in refining both the content and the delivery of your mini-course. Think of it as your testing phase before you go full throttle.

Simplify the Format

The best mini-courses are short, actionable, and easy to consume. Aim for under an hour of total content, divided into digestible chunks. It's far better to have a series of short, compelling lessons than one long, overwhelming feature.

It's like a Netflix series—people are more likely to binge-watch a show with short episodes than sit down for a 3-hour movie. Keep your content concise, and your students will stay engaged.

Price It to Validate

Your mini-course doesn't have to be priced high to be valuable. In fact, you should price it at a low introductory rate, somewhere around $17 or $47. The goal here is validation. You want to prove that people are willing to pay for your expertise.

Think of it like setting up a lemonade stand before you open a full-scale juice bar. You're testing the market with minimal investment before diving in. Once you've validated the demand, you can adjust the price as you build credibility and gain testimonials.

Market with Transformation in Mind

When it's time to promote your mini-course, don't focus on what's inside it. Focus on the transformation it provides. Your audience isn't interested in how many modules or worksheets you have. They want to know how their life will improve after they finish the course.

Instead of saying, "This course covers gut health," say, "By the end, you'll have a 7-day plan to reduce bloating and improve digestion."

As the saying goes, "Sell the destination, not the journey." Your audience cares about where you're taking them, not the vehicle you're using to get there. Focus on the result, and they'll be ready to sign up.

Today's Exercise: Craft Your Mini-Course

Let's get hands-on. You're going to create a step-by-step outline for your mini-course. The goal is to act on what we've covered. We want to build a focused, actionable course that solves a specific problem for your audience.

Follow these steps:

1. **Identify a Specific Problem**

   ○ Write down one niche-specific problem your audience struggles with. Keep it short and actionable. Example: "How to reduce stress in 7 days for busy professionals."

2. **Frame the Transformation**

   ○ What's the "before" state your audience is in? What are they frustrated or confused about? Then, write down the "after" state. What will they feel or experience once they've completed your course?

   ○ Example: "Before: Overwhelmed and stressed out. After: Confident, calm, and in control."

3. **Break It Into 3-5 Steps**

   ○ Think of 3-5 actionable steps that will help your audience move from "before" to "after." These steps will become your mini-course modules. Make sure each step is specific and clear.

   ○ Example: "Step 1: Eliminate processed sugars from your diet."

4. **Simplify Each Step**

   ○ For each step, write down a quick lesson plan. It could be a short video or a simple worksheet, but the key is to keep it focused and actionable.

   ○ Ask yourself, "What does my audience need to *do* to make progress?"

5. Ask for Feedback

- Before you launch your mini-course, pick 3-5 people who fit your ideal audience and offer them early access. Ask for honest feedback: What was clear? What was confusing? Would they pay for this?

6. Set a Price

- Pick a low introductory price. Don't overthink it. The goal is to validate that people are willing to pay for this solution.

- Example: "I'll price my mini-course at $27 to start."

7. Create a Short Promotion

- Write a one-paragraph description of your course that focuses on the transformation. Highlight what your students will achieve, not just what's inside the course.

- Example: "In just 7 days, you'll learn simple strategies to reduce stress and reclaim your calm, no matter how busy your schedule is."

Complete these steps, and you'll have a clear, actionable outline for your mini-course that's ready to validate with your audience.

Key Takeaways:

- Start small to validate: A mini-course tests your market and refines your message. It does so without overcommitting time or resources.

- Focus on transformation, not information: Your audience

wants a clear before-and-after outcome, not just more content.

- Act fast: Make a simple, niche course. Get quick feedback to check if you're meeting real needs before scaling.

14

The Teacher's Main Offer: A Flagship Course

I couldn't believe it. I sat staring at my email, reading the words that would change everything: "You've received $97 in your Pay-Pal account." Minutes later, it happened again. By the end of the weekend, over 15 emails had rolled in, each one announcing a new customer who had enrolled in my job search course. For the first time, I experienced what my mentor, Dan Miller, had been teaching me—the power of *Swiss dollars.*

What are Swiss dollars? It's simple: sales while I sleep soundly. My small career coaching site for accountants had begun to earn money, whether I was working or not. I had bottled up seven years of experience as an executive recruiter into an online course, and it was doing the heavy lifting for me.

It's a surreal feeling knowing that you're teaching someone how to get a better job without actually being there to teach them. After that weekend, I was hooked. The course creation bug had bitten me, and it wouldn't let go. For the past 13 years, I've built and launched multiple online courses, each one allowing me to reach more people while giving me back my time.

That's what this chapter is about—how to create your own flagship course. The course will take all your expertise and years of experience and package it into something scalable. It's the key to breaking free from trading time for money. When done right, this course won't just help your audience; it'll transform your business and your life.

Let's dive into why this shift is so powerful and how you can get started on the same journey.

Trading Time for Dollars

Most people in coaching or consulting fall into a familiar pattern. They exchange their time for dollars. It seems like the obvious choice when you've built up experience and expertise. You charge by the hour or for sessions, and your clients get personalized attention. It feels productive because you're busy, and your clients are happy. But here's the catch: no matter how much you charge, you're still tied to the clock.

Each hour is a block you can never get back. And because time is limited, so is your income. You can only take on so many clients in a week. Want to make more money? You have to either raise your rates or work more hours. But there's only so much time in a day, and the thought of working more, of cramming in extra clients, starts to feel like a grind. The hustle culture tells you to push harder. But harder work doesn't equal bigger results.

This cycle leads to burnout. You're giving more and more of yourself, but the ceiling on your income doesn't budge. It's exhausting, and deep down, you know it's unsustainable. Every hour you spend working is an hour you're not spending on anything else—your family, your hobbies, your own health. And when you're done with that session or call? The money stops. There's no residual benefit from the work you put in.

The Ceiling on Income and Impact

The time-for-dollars model might seem like the safest option, but it comes with serious limitations. First, there's an undeniable cap on your income. There are only so many hours in a day, and no matter how much you love your work, you can't stretch time.

That means you're stuck. Even if you're at your maximum rate, your income is boxed in. It's frustrating because you want to grow. You've worked hard to get where you are, but the financial freedom you're after always feels just out of reach.

Then there's the flexibility issue. You're constantly tethered to the clock. You can't take a day off without losing income. You can't travel or even get sick without it hitting your bottom line. It creates this dependency on being *always available* and adds pressure to be "on" all the time. You may have started your business for freedom. But, you've built yourself another job. You're both the boss and the employee, and neither gets a break.

Emotionally, this approach wears you down. You love helping people, but constantly juggling time and energy between clients leaves you drained. The thought of scaling your business feels impossible because you can't physically do more. And while your passion drives you, the frustration of knowing there's a ceiling above you is hard to shake.

Why You Need to Build a Flagship Course

A flagship course changes the game. Instead of serving clients one by one, you serve them all at once. This isn't just about scaling—it's about multiplying your impact. Your flagship course is the vehicle that shares your best knowledge with thousands. It does this without you having to show up every time.

When you create a flagship course, you're no longer trading time for dollars. You're creating something that works for you—whether you're in the room or not. It bottles up your experience, your wisdom, and your insights into a structured format that people can access whenever they need it. It's a way of teaching without having to be present. And that's where the magic happens.

Think of your flagship course as your legacy. It's the culmination of everything you've learned, packaged in a way that creates lasting value. Once it's built, it works for you, day and night. Your course becomes the key that unlocks the door to scaling both your income and your impact. You're no longer limited by the hours in a day or the energy you have to give. Instead, you're free to focus on other areas of your business—or your life—while your course continues to serve others.

That's the shift from constantly hustling to creating something that gives back to you. This is what allows you to scale without burning out. You're building an asset, not just selling your time.

The Freedom and Flexibility of Course Creation

An online course opens the door to a level of freedom that's hard to find anywhere else. Instead of repeating the same lessons with each client, you record your best knowledge once. Then, share it with as many people as you want. That's the power of online courses. You can serve hundreds, even thousands, with the same content while you're free to focus on what matters most to you.

Imagine waking up and knowing your course is working. Students are learning, progress is happening, and income is flowing in—all while you do other things. You might be working on a big project. Or, you could be spending time with family. Maybe you're exploring a passion that doesn't pay but fulfills you. Course creation gives you back control over your time. It shifts your focus from trading hours for dollars to building assets that continue to provide long after the work is done.

With online courses, your reach isn't limited to geography. You can tap into a global audience—someone in London can learn from you just as easily as someone in your own hometown. This dramatically expands your potential impact. You're no longer constrained by who can physically meet with you. And because your course lives online, it can scale infinitely. Whether ten people sign up or ten thousand, the course delivers the same value without you having to lift a finger after it's built. That's the beauty of passive income—money that works for you while you focus on creating more value elsewhere.

Leveraging Your Expertise to Help More People

An online course isn't just a way to earn more; it's a way to help more people. When you bottle up your expertise into a flagship course, you're amplifying your ability to serve. Instead of helping one person at a time, you're creating a ripple effect. Your knowledge spreads, reaching people who might never have been able to work with you one-on-one.

Your knowledge is valuable. People are searching for exactly what you know, but it has to be delivered in a way that's structured, accessible, and transformative. It's not enough to dump everything you know into a course and call it a day. Your course needs to guide your audience through a journey. Every lesson should build toward a result they want to achieve, whether that's a new skill, a mindset shift, or a solution to a problem they're facing.

When you create a flagship course that truly serves people, it builds trust. You become the authority in your niche—not because you say so, but because your course delivers. You've positioned yourself as the go-to expert, and your audience sees you as someone who can help them achieve real transformation. This is how you not only scale your income but also scale your impact. The more people you help, the more your reputation grows. It becomes a cycle where you're known for delivering results, and that attracts even more people to your course.

And here's the thing: as your course helps more people, it also frees you up to continue refining your expertise. You're not bogged down with day-to-day client work. You can think bigger, innovate, and find new ways to provide value.

Today's Exercise: Start Designing Your Flagship Course

Your flagship course might feel overwhelming at first. But breaking it into steps makes it easier to tackle. Here's a simple step-by-step action plan to help you start designing your course today.

Step 1: Define Your Target Audience

Start by getting crystal clear on who your course is for. Write down who you want to serve. Think about the specific group of people that will benefit most from your expertise. What's the big problem they're facing that your course will help them solve? Be specific. The clearer you are about your audience, the better you can craft a course that speaks directly to their needs.

Ask yourself:

- What keeps them up at night?

- What are their goals or frustrations?

- How will this course make their lives better?

Step 2: Outline Your Expertise

Now it's time to list out the major topics or lessons from your own experience that will form the backbone of your course. Think about the top 3-5 things your audience needs to know to achieve the transformation they're after. These will become the core content of your course. Don't get bogged down with details just yet—this is a high-level view.

For example:

- If you're a career coach, your lessons might include "How to Ace the Interview" or "Building a Personal Brand."

- If you're in health and fitness, you might focus on "Creating a Sustainable Workout Plan" or "Nutrition Basics for Busy Professionals."

Step 3: Craft Your Course Promise

Every course needs a promise—what your students will gain by the time they finish. This is the transformation you're offering. Write a single, clear sentence that explains what your course will help them achieve.

For example:

- "By the end of this course, you will have built a clear, actionable plan to land your dream job."

- "By the end of this course, you'll know how to create and

stick to a sustainable fitness routine."

Keep it simple and outcome-focused. This promise will guide everything else you create.

Step 4: Map Out Your Course Structure

Next, break your course down into modules and lessons. Each module should cover one major topic, and each lesson should dive into a specific subtopic within that module. Your course outline should look something like this:

- **Module 1: Introduction to Personal Branding**

  - Lesson 1: Understanding Your Unique Value

  - Lesson 2: Crafting Your Elevator Pitch

- **Module 2: Mastering Job Interviews**

  - Lesson 1: Common Interview Questions

  - Lesson 2: Creating a Winning Resume

Don't worry about making it perfect right now. Just get a rough structure in place. You can always refine it later.

Step 5: Identify a Platform

There are many platforms where you can host your course, so it's important to find one that fits your needs and budget. Some popular options include Teachable, Kajabi, and Thinkific. Look for a platform that's easy to use, offers good support, and provides the features you need, like video hosting, quizzes, or student tracking.

Take some time to research:

- What's your budget?

- Do you need advanced features like memberships or email integrations?

- How tech-savvy are you, and how much support will you need?

Step 6: Set a Launch Date

The final step is to set a deadline for launching your course. Pick a realistic date that gives you enough time to create the content, but don't give yourself too much room to procrastinate. A deadline creates accountability and keeps you on track.

Mark it on your calendar, and make a commitment to yourself to follow through. If it helps, break it down into smaller milestones, like finishing one module per week.

By following these steps, you'll go from having an idea for a course to having a solid plan. Keep things simple, focus on the essentials, and remember: Done is better than perfect.

Key Takeaways:

- Online courses let you stop trading time for dollars. By creating a flagship course, you can package your knowledge. It will generate income without constant work.

- A flagship course unlocks scale. It lets you teach and serve many people at once, not just one-on-one clients. This will boost your impact and allow for rapid growth.

- Your flagship course is the key to long-term, sustainable income. Once created, your course can earn money for years. It will provide financial security and freedom.

15

The Teacher's Max Offer: A Membership Site

W hen I started my first membership site, I didn't really know what I was doing. My email list was small, and I wasn't even sure if a membership was something I wanted to commit to. So, I decided to try a little experiment. I opened the doors to just 50 people. I called them charter members, charged them $20 a month, and let them know they were getting in on something new. They would help me shape this thing as it grew. Once I hit 50, I shut the doors.

Those first 50 members felt like a huge win. But what happened next surprised me even more. By the time I reopened a month later, I already had a waitlist of people eager to get in. So, I bumped the price up to $25 and repeated the process. Opened the doors, hit 50 members, closed it again. Within 90 days, I had around 150 people paying me monthly. And just like that, I was making about $3,000 a month in recurring revenue.

Here's the thing—I wasn't launching new products, running ads, or hustling nonstop. Instead, I was building something sustainable. A membership site gave me recurring income, and the best part was, it grew over time without me constantly chasing new sales. That experiment turned into a peaceful, predictable business model.

This chapter is about the power of that kind of stability. A membership site isn't just a way to make money—it's a way to create consistent, reliable income while deepening your connection with your audience. Let's explore why this model works so well and how it can change everything for your business.

How Most People Approach Memberships

When most people think of starting a membership site, they treat it like a one-time product sale. They build out a massive library of content, imagining that if they just keep piling more in, members will stick around. They focus on quantity, believing that more options, more videos, and more resources must equal more value. It's a common trap.

The reality? Cramming in too much content often leads to overwhelm. Members sign up, they log in, and they see this mountain of resources they're supposed to climb. It's too much. They can't keep up, and when that happens, the perceived value plummets. Instead of feeling supported, they feel stressed. Instead of staying, they leave.

Most people also rely heavily on single launches to fill their memberships. You see it all the time. Open the doors with a big splash, close them again, and then... silence. This rollercoaster creates instability. The high of a big launch is exciting, but as soon as the doors close, the income dries up. It's an exhausting cycle, and without a plan for what happens in between, you're stuck waiting for the next big push to bring in new members.

The Hidden Pitfalls of This Strategy

Overwhelming members with too much content leads to cancellations. It's counterintuitive, but it's true. People want clarity, not chaos. They don't want a flood of information they'll never get through. They want guidance, a clear path forward, and a feeling of accomplishment as they move through the material. When members feel behind, they quit.

Relying on single launches to drive membership also creates a feast-or-famine situation. You're either riding the wave of a successful launch, or you're dealing with the slow, painful decline of attrition. It's a model built on hype rather than long-term stability, and it forces you into a constant cycle of selling. The pressure to always have the next launch ready can burn you out fast.

How to Build a Better Membership Model

The solution is to create a peaceful system that delivers consistent, manageable value each month. Think of it as building a rhythm. Instead of overwhelming your members with too much content all at once, offer 1-2 key pieces of content each month that align with their needs. Each piece should move them closer to their goal, keeping them engaged without overwhelming them.

This approach also eliminates the pressure of relying on launches. Instead of closing your membership after each big event, you shift to an evergreen model. It's always open and steadily growing. Members join when they're ready, and you can attract them with specific, high-interest content.

It's like how streaming services work. Netflix doesn't just say, "Join to get access to our entire catalog." Instead, they hook you with a specific show or movie that fits your interests. You sign up for one thing, but you stay because the value keeps coming. Your membership can work the same way. Use targeted offers that solve immediate problems to attract people. Then, keep them by delivering useful, engaging content.

Focus on Monthly Value Rhythms

Membership sites thrive on consistency, not volume. Instead of overwhelming your members with a flood of content, give them something they can actually use. Structure your membership around manageable monthly deliverables. This could be a masterclass, a live workshop, or a downloadable playbook—whatever fits your niche. The key is to offer 1-2 core pieces of content each month. These should align with a clear path that leads members from where they are to where they want to be.

When people know what's coming each month, they feel supported, not overwhelmed. It creates a rhythm they can depend on, and that rhythm keeps them engaged.

Create a Success Path Framework

Your members need more than random resources—they need direction. A success path framework is like a roadmap. It shows members how to get from point A to point B. Without it, they can feel lost. They won't know what to focus on or how to measure their progress. A clear framework provides structure. It shows them exactly what they need to do next. Each deliverable you provide should support that framework, helping your members move forward step by step.

This framework not only guides them but also builds trust. When members see results, they stick around.

Shift to Evergreen Promotions

Big launches are exciting but unsustainable. An evergreen membership model—where people can join at any time—gives you steady, predictable growth. With evergreen promotions, you don't rely on that one huge push to get people through the door. Instead, you can focus on attracting members consistently in smaller but more sustainable numbers.

Think of it like having an "always-open" sign on your business. Members can join when they're ready, and you're not caught in the frantic cycle of launch after launch.

Keep It Simple, Not Overwhelming

One of the biggest mistakes people make with memberships is trying to offer too much. More content doesn't mean more value—it often means overwhelm. Less is more. By offering just one or two core resources each month, you give your members the chance to actually implement what they've learned. They don't feel like they're falling behind. Instead, they feel empowered to make progress.

Your goal is to provide clarity, not chaos.

Use Scarcity and Urgency in Small Doses

Scarcity and urgency are powerful, but they don't need to be used all the time. Instead of constant relaunches, use limited-time offers. They create urgency and nudge people to act. You can still create excitement without making it a full-blown event every time. A well-timed offer creates that little push some people need to finally join without exhausting you or your audience.

When used sparingly, scarcity feels natural—not forced.

Today's Exercise: Creating Your Success Path

A clear success path is the backbone of any membership. It gives your members direction and helps them feel like they're making real progress. Let's create your success path.

1. **Define the Transformation.** Start by asking yourself: *What's the end result I want my members to achieve?* This is the transformation your membership promises. Whether it's helping them write a book, build an online business, or improve their health, get clear on the big outcome. Write it down in one sentence. For example: "My membership helps aspiring authors finish and self-publish their first book."

2. **Break Down the Journey.** Now, break that transformation into 3-7 stages. Think of these as milestones your members need to hit along the way. Each stage should feel like progress, giving them a sense of accomplishment as they move through the membership. These stages should be simple, logical steps. For example, a membership for authors might have stages like:

   ◦ Finding their book idea

   ◦ Creating a writing routine

   ◦ Completing the first draft

   ◦ Preparing for self-publishing

3. **Name the Stages.** Give each stage a clear, descriptive name. It helps your members understand where they are in the process and what's coming next. Try to make these names action-oriented and specific. For example:

- "Discover Your Book Idea"

- "Build Your Writing Habit"

- "Finish Your First Draft"

4. **Assign Monthly Deliverables.** For each stage, think of what resources or content you can provide to help your members move forward. Assign 1-2 monthly deliverables to each stage. These could be tutorials, worksheets, or live workshops. Make sure each deliverable directly supports the stage it's connected to. For example:

   - In "Discover Your Book Idea," your deliverables might be a brainstorming worksheet and a video lesson on finding your niche.

5. **Map the Path for Your Members.** Put it all together in a visual format. Create a simple roadmap or success path graphic that shows your members how they'll progress through the membership. Each stage should flow into the next, and your deliverables should be clearly linked to the path. This helps members see the journey ahead and gives them a sense of structure and purpose.

With your success path, your members will have a clear, guided experience. It will make them confident about staying and completing their journey.

Key Takeaways:

- **Recurring revenue is the lifeblood of sustainable business growth.** A well-structured membership site creates a stable income stream and frees you from constant sales pressure.

- **Less is more**. Don't overwhelm your members. Deliver a few, high-value resources each month. They should align with a clear success path.

- **Think evergreen**. Use an open-enrollment model. It lets new members join at any time. Support it with occasional promotions for urgency. Don't rely on large-scale launches.

16

The Speaker's Mini Offer: A Paid Virtual Workshop

I n 1984, TED began as an exclusive conference. It brought together the top minds in technology, entertainment, and design to share long, in-depth talks. For years, these talks were available only to those who could attend the conference in person. But in 2006, TED did something revolutionary. They took their talks online and made them available to everyone for free. They also introduced a key change—each talk would be no longer than 18 minutes.

That decision changed the game. It proved that a speaker didn't need an hour or even 30 minutes to make an impact. In fact, short, focused talks often left a stronger impression. TED Talks became a global phenomenon, proving that powerful ideas could be communicated in a short amount of time and still pack a punch. It was the shift from long-winded lectures to bite-sized presentations that captured the world's attention.

This evolution mirrors a powerful lesson for today's aspiring speakers. You don't need to wait for a big stage or a lengthy spotlight to deliver value. Hosting your own virtual workshops allows you to present your ideas in a concise, engaging format, much like a TED Talk. Short, impactful sessions not only keep your audience engaged but also open the door to paid opportunities.[6]

Like TED transformed the speaking world, you can create your own stage through virtual workshops. There, powerful, bite-sized content can deeply resonate with your audience and get you paid for your expertise.

The Waiting Game

Many aspiring speakers follow the same path. They send out dozens of applications. They network, hoping to get noticed. They wait for an organization or event to offer them a stage. It's a passive approach, depending on someone else to open the door. Some speakers wait for years, hustling to build their reputation and hoping for a chance to finally get paid for their expertise.

But even when they get the opportunity, the payoff isn't always great. A lot of initial speaking gigs don't come with a paycheck. At best, they might cover travel expenses or offer "exposure." That exposure might help you build credibility over time. But, it often frustrates speakers. They feel like they're spinning their wheels without real results.

Why That Approach Falls Flat

Relying on someone else to give you a platform puts you in a long line of other hopefuls. It means you're constantly competing for limited spots with little control over your own career. The slow climb to recognition through unpaid or low-paying gigs often leads to burnout. Many speakers give up before they even get a chance to hit their stride.

Plus, the truth is that exposure doesn't pay the bills. Even after securing a speaking opportunity, the financial rewards are often underwhelming. By waiting for others to give you a stage, you're missing out on the chance to take control of your speaking career from the start.

How to Flip the Script

You don't have to wait for someone to hand you a microphone. The best way to get paid to speak is to create your own platform. Hosting a paid virtual workshop puts you in the driver's seat. You get to decide the topic, the audience, and the price. Instead of waiting for exposure, you can monetize your expertise directly and immediately. Virtual workshops also offer scalability. You can reach people from all over the world, and once you have the structure in place, you can run it multiple times with different audiences.

This shift isn't just about getting paid; it's about creating an avenue for recurring income. When you take control of your platform, you control your success.

Steps to Create a Successful Paid Virtual Workshop

Choose a Focus for Your Workshop

Your workshop can't be everything to everyone. To stand out, it's crucial to narrow down your topic. Instead of offering something broad like "Public Speaking," get specific. Choose a niche focus that solves a particular problem your audience is facing. For example, "How to Captivate Your Audience in 5 Minutes or Less" solves a specific problem. It appeals to those who need that solution. When you specialize, you create a clear, targeted path for your audience, making it easier for them to see the value in what you're offering.

A river cuts through rock, not because of its power, but because of its persistence. Just like a narrow river creates a deep impact, narrowing your workshop allows you to dive deep into solving one clear issue for your audience. This kind of focus makes your workshop not just another option, but *the* solution.

Break Your Content into Digestible Chunks

Once you've defined your niche, it's time to structure your content in a way that keeps your audience engaged. People don't respond well to long, drawn-out lectures. Break your workshop into bite-sized segments—15 to 20 minutes each is ideal. Each segment should tackle one key point, giving participants time to absorb the information before moving on to the next.

Teaching is like feeding your audience. Give them too much at once, and they'll choke. Serve it in courses, and they'll savor each bite. Smaller content chunks prevent overload. They keep participants engaged and eager to learn.

Make It Interactive with Applied Exercises

Learning is an active process, not a passive one. After each teaching segment, give your audience the chance to apply what they've just learned. These exercises reinforce the material and help participants feel more confident in their ability to use it. You could include activities like worksheets, group discussions, or brainstorming. Practical exercises keep the learning experience hands-on and make your content stick.

"Tell me, and I forget. Teach me, and I remember. Involve me, and I learn." —Benjamin Franklin. When participants can apply knowledge immediately, they absorb it more deeply.

Incorporate Breakout Sessions to Foster Connection

Virtual workshops don't have to feel impersonal. You can use tools like Zoom breakout rooms to divide your participants into smaller groups. This encourages intimate discussions, collaboration, and deeper connections. Breakout sessions work well after you've covered much material. They let participants digest and reflect on the content together.

Learning together in small groups creates bonds that turn knowledge into community wisdom. By creating space for your audience to engage with each other, you add value and make the experience more memorable.

Make Time for Q&A Sessions

It's essential to give your audience a chance to ask questions throughout your workshop. After every major section, dedicate time to a Q&A session. This helps participants clarify any doubts they have and allows you to gauge their understanding of the material. It's also a great way for participants to personalize their experience and feel more connected to the content.

"Questions are the engines of intellect. They convert energy to motion and curiosity to inquiry." —David Hackett Fischer. A well-timed Q&A turns your workshop from a one-way lecture into an interactive conversation.

End with an Actionable Summary

The last step of your workshop should leave participants with a clear path forward. Summarize the main points and offer actionable next steps. Your goal is to ensure that participants leave feeling confident and motivated. So, provide extra resources, an invite to a follow-up, or tips for applying what they learned. A strong conclusion cements your workshop's value. It keeps your audience engaged after the session ends.

The journey of a thousand miles begins with a single step. Your workshop is the first step in that journey for your audience. Clear, actionable advice at the end will help. It will make participants more likely to apply what they've learned. That's where the real transformation begins.

Today's Exercise: Craft Your First Paid Virtual Workshop

1. **Brainstorm Your Workshop Topic.** Write down three topics you're passionate about and knowledgeable about. Now, think about the specific problems your audience faces. Narrow each topic down into something more focused. For example, if you're an expert in digital marketing, use "How to Run a Successful Facebook Ad Campaign with $100," not "Digital Marketing Basics." Choose the most compelling, practical topic to solve in a short workshop.

2. **Break Down Your Content into Chunks.** With your topic in mind, break it into smaller parts. Aim for three to five key sections that could each be taught in 15- to 20-minute chunks. For each section, write a short bullet point list of what you'll cover. Remember, the goal is to keep each section focused on one core idea. For example, if you're teaching about Facebook ads, one section could be "Understanding Your Target Audience."

3. **Create One Interactive Exercise for Each Section.** Go back

to each section and think of an exercise that helps participants apply what they've just learned. It could be a worksheet, a brief discussion, or an individual task. If a section is about targeting Facebook ads, ask participants to define their ideal customer and write down three interests for ad targeting. Write down one practical exercise for each section you've created.

4. **Plan Your Breakout Sessions.** Decide where in your workshop you'll use breakout sessions. Write down at least one prompt or discussion question for each breakout session. For example, after teaching about ad targeting, group the participants. Have them share their targeting ideas and get feedback. These breakout sessions will allow for peer learning and connection.

5. **Design Your Q&A Times.** Now, look at your sections and decide where to place a few short Q&A breaks. Mark those spots on your outline. Think about common questions you expect participants to ask and jot down some answers to prepare. This will help you manage time and keep the Q&A sessions flowing smoothly.

6. **Wrap It Up with Clear Action Steps.** After your last teaching segment, plan to end your workshop with an actionable summary. Write down three clear steps that participants can take immediately after the workshop to implement what they've learned. Whether it's a link to a resource, a worksheet, or an invite to a follow-up session, ensure participants leave with a sense of direction.

This process will give you a clear structure for your paid virtual workshop. It will also give you a plan to deliver value to your audience.

Key Takeaways:

- Hosting a paid virtual workshop lets you control your platform. It also creates income without waiting for opportunities.

- Breaking content into focused, bite-sized chunks keeps your audience engaged and maximizes learning.

- Interactive exercises and Q&A sessions build connections. They help participants apply what they've learned right away.

17

The Speaker's Main Offer: Paid Speaking Gigs

There I was, holding a check for several thousand dollars. I'd just wrapped up a 45-minute speech, and to top it off, my flight, food, and transportation were all covered. I couldn't believe it—I had actually been paid to speak. It felt surreal.

But the money wasn't even the best part. I got to spend a few days surrounded by amazing people, traveling to a state I'd never visited before. I even had time to do a little sightseeing. The whole experience felt like a dream, one of those moments you secretly hope for but don't expect to happen. And yet, there I was. Paid to speak, to share what I knew, and to enjoy the process along the way.

It hadn't always been this way. I'd given plenty of talks for free—talks where I had to pay for my own coffee, let alone my travel. But that was part of the journey, and looking back, I wouldn't trade it. Those unpaid gigs were stepping stones, building blocks that got me to where I am now, standing on a stage with people eager to listen.

In this chapter, we're going to break down the essentials that'll prepare you for your first paid speaking gig. Because, let's face it, you don't just show up one day and get handed a check. There's the groundwork that needs to be laid—things you need to have in place long before you ever step on stage. The good news? It's simpler than you think when you know what really matters.

Where Most Speakers Get Stuck

Aspiring speakers often feel overwhelmed by all the advice out there. It seems like everyone has an opinion on what it takes to make it as a speaker. So, they spend their time focusing on things that seem important but aren't. They might obsess over their website, promo materials, or a perfect speaking bio. All the while, they hope these things will somehow lead to being "discovered." Maybe an event planner will stumble across their website and invite them to speak at a big conference. Or maybe they send out cold pitches, waiting for someone to reply. But nothing happens.

The truth is, most of that stuff won't land you paid gigs. And it's easy to fall into the trap of thinking, "If I just get these pieces perfect, the opportunities will come." The result? A lot of energy is spent on things that don't actually move the needle. No matter how polished your website looks or how fancy your promo materials are, none of that guarantees you'll get hired.

Why This Strategy Leaves You Speaking to Empty Rooms

Spending time on the wrong things leads to frustration. You're spinning your wheels, but you're not getting any traction. A polished website or a detailed bio may seem like progress. But, if you're not building relationships or crafting a clear, resonant message, those efforts are wasted.

Cold pitching rarely works because it lacks connection. When you're sending emails into the void, event planners don't know you, and they don't have a reason to trust you. Even if you're offering to speak for free, it doesn't always open the door to bigger opportunities. In the end, many speakers end up stuck—still doing unpaid gigs or settling for low-paying events that don't lead to more.

How to Get on the Main Stage

It's time to stop chasing the wrong things. What really works? Building a speaker's toolbox that sets you up for success. Instead of worrying about all the little details, focus on the few things that matter most. There's a small group of speakers—the top 20%—who consistently land paid gigs. These speakers know that it's not about having the flashiest website or the longest list of accomplishments. It's about having a clear message, building relationships, and making yourself easy to work with.

So, how do you get there? Start by narrowing down your speaking topics to a few clear, focused keynotes that speak directly to your audience. You also need a system for generating leads so you're not just waiting for opportunities to find you. And finally, you need a solid speaker contract that protects you and ensures you're compensated fairly.

When you shift your focus to these essentials, you'll start seeing results. Instead of getting bogged down in the things that don't matter, you'll be ready for the right opportunities when they come your way.

Craft Keynotes That Hit Home

The first thing you need is a solid lineup of keynotes. These aren't just random topics thrown together—they should come straight from your framework. Think about the problems your audience faces and the solutions you offer. Your keynotes should speak directly to those pain points. You're not here to give a generic, one-size-fits-all talk. Each keynote should feel tailor-made for the audience, even if you're using the same content across different events.

For example, if you've developed a framework for overcoming mind-set blocks, you can adjust the message depending on the audience. At a podcasting conference, you might talk about "The Five Mind-sets Successful Podcasters Need." At a corporate event, that same framework could become "Breaking Through Mental Barriers to Leadership." It has the same core message but is adapted to meet the needs of the crowd. The goal is to create 2 to 3 keynotes that align with your audience's struggles and goals so you can confidently present them at different events.

Build a Lead Machine

Paid speaking gigs don't just fall into your lap. You need to go out and find them. This is where having a lead generation system comes in. The goal is to actively seek out opportunities rather than waiting for them to come to you. Start by researching conferences in your niche. You can easily find events by typing "conference + [your niche]" into Google. Create a database with key details. It should have event names, dates, locations, and, most importantly, contact info for decision-makers.

This isn't a one-time thing. You'll need to update your list regularly and continue reaching out to new event organizers. But having this system in place makes it so much easier to consistently find potential gigs. Without it, you're just guessing—and that leads to missed opportunities.

Lock It Down with a Contract

There's nothing worse than landing a gig only to find out you're not getting paid what you expected or that the organizer flakes on you at the last minute. That's where a speaker contract comes in. This isn't just a nice-to-have; it's essential. Your contract should set clear expectations. It should include your speaking fee and a 50% non-refundable deposit upfront.

Why a deposit? It secures your time and ensures you won't be left hanging if plans change. Plus, it covers any travel or accommodation expenses, so you're not out of pocket. A contract not only protects you but also sends a message: you're a professional. You're serious about your craft, and you expect to be treated as such. This foundation of professionalism will pay off in the long run by ensuring smooth experiences and repeat bookings.

Be a Breeze to Work With

Event planners are juggling a thousand details, and the last thing they need is a difficult speaker. You want to be the easiest person on their list. Keep your requests simple. Don't make complicated demands for special treatment or a long list of requirements. Handle your own travel and accommodations without a fuss. The easier you are to work with, the more likely they'll be to invite you back or recommend you to other event planners.

Word travels fast in these circles. If you're known as someone who delivers value without causing headaches, you'll be the first person they think of when they need a reliable speaker. Make their job easy, and you'll find that doors open much more quickly.

Deliver Talks That Lead to Results

Great keynotes don't just inspire—they move people to action. Event organizers want speakers who can provide more than just feel-good moments. They want results. Your framework should provide clear, actionable takeaways. The audience must be able to use them right away. Whether it's a mindset shift, a new strategy, or a practical tool, make sure you're giving your audience something concrete.

When you can consistently deliver value that leads to real results, you'll stand out from the crowd. Event planners will remember that your talks don't just entertain—they make a measurable difference for the attendees. And that's exactly what they want to see.

Today's Exercise: Craft Your 3 Signature Talks

Let's get your signature talks locked in. Follow these steps to create keynotes that align with your message and resonate with your audience.

1. **Identify Your Core Message.** Start by thinking about your overall message. What do you stand for? What's the common thread in your teachings, whether you're writing, coaching, or speaking? Write down a few sentences that capture the essence of what you want to share with the world. This will be the foundation of your keynotes.

2. **Pinpoint Audience Pain Points.** Consider the struggles your audience faces. What keeps them up at night? What challenges are they trying to overcome? List at least 3-5 common pain points your audience consistently deals with. This list will help you tailor your talks to hit home with your listeners.

3. **Match Your Framework to the Struggles.** Review your framework. Which parts of it directly address the struggles you've identified? Circle or highlight 2-3 sections of your framework that align with these pain points. These sections will serve as the core of your signature talks.

4. **Write Out Potential Titles.** Brainstorm titles for your talks. These should be punchy and clear. Aim for titles that immediately tell the audience what they'll gain from your presentation. For example, if your framework covers productivity, a title could be "The 3 Productivity Hacks High Performers Swear By." Come up with 2-3 titles for each signature talk. Choose the one that feels the strongest.

5. **Outline Your Talks.** For each keynote, outline the main points you'll cover. Don't worry about every little detail yet—just focus on the core ideas. Jot down 3-5 bullet points for each talk, hitting on the major takeaways you want your audience to leave with.

By the end of this exercise, you'll have three well-defined talks ready to present at any event, tailored to the needs of your ideal audience.

Key Takeaways:

- Paid speaking gigs require three key strategies. First, deliver impactful keynotes. Second, create a lead-generation system. Lastly, clear agreements with a speaker contract must be secured.

- Most aspiring speakers focus on non-essential tasks. Instead, build a speaker's toolbox. It should be results-oriented. This will prepare you for the right opportunity when it arises.

- Being the easiest speaker to work with builds relationships with event planners. It will get you invited back and referred for future opportunities.

18

The Speaker's Max Offer: Host In-Person Events

"Don't tell anybody, but I would pay them to do this." Those were the words my co-host said to me right before we walked into the room for my first in-person event. I remember it like it was yesterday. The year was 2015, and hosting an in-person event had been a dream of mine for a long time. As a former high school teacher, I always loved the energy and interaction of being in front of a live audience. But there were so many hurdles.

My business was mainly online, and my audience was spread out across the country. How was I going to get them all to one place? Where should I host the event? How much would it cost? Should I provide transportation from the airport? Would anyone even come? And what about the food and drinks? Every time I thought I was ready to dive in, another logistical question popped up, and I found myself hesitating.

Luckily, I had a partner who'd done this a hundred times before. Dennis made it all seem possible. We decided to keep it simple—just 15 people for a 3-day event. Small enough to manage but meaningful enough to make an impact. We charged a few thousand dollars to attend, and that small group was exactly the nudge I needed to start something bigger.

Fast forward to today, and every year I host a larger event with both in-person and virtual tickets. It's become easier with each event, not because logistics got simpler, but because I stopped doing what didn't work and focused on what did.

In this chapter, I'll share what I've learned from years of hosting events. You'll learn best practices, common pitfalls, and strategies. They can help you host your own paid in-person events without feeling overwhelmed.

The Common Missteps of Event Hosting

It's easy to get caught up in the excitement of hosting your first event. Most speakers make the mistake of thinking bigger is better. They try to fill a convention center or fancy hotel ballroom with large-scale gatherings, without considering the cost. Venues like these come with hefty food and AV expenses that quickly add up.

Another common misstep is assuming more people will show up than actually do. It's tempting to dream of packed rooms, but without building a core audience first, that dream often falls short. Speakers also tend to overlook the real money-making opportunities at events. They focus too much on ticket sales and forget the value of offering upsells like coaching, courses, or other products.

The Problem with Going Big Too Soon

The reality is that scaling too fast comes with its own set of problems. Hosting large events without experience can easily lead to financial loss. Expensive venues and over-the-top budgets quickly eat away at any potential profits.

But the pressure doesn't stop there. Managing a big crowd is stressful. You must juggle complex logistics and ensure everything runs smoothly. It's enough to make anyone feel overwhelmed. Worst of all, larger events often sacrifice the deep connections that can be made in smaller, more intimate settings. The kind of connections that build trust and loyalty.

A Smarter Strategy

The better approach is to think small, at least in the beginning. Start with a smaller event and scale up gradually as you learn the ropes. Instead of going for hundreds of attendees, aim for an intimate group of 10 to 20 people. This allows you to focus on meaningful interactions rather than managing chaos.

Capping ticket sales at a smaller number also lets you charge a premium. Attendees will gladly pay more for a personal experience where they feel seen and heard. Choosing a simpler venue that minimizes costs and logistics will also keep things manageable.

The key isn't to try and make a huge profit from your first event. Break even if you can, and look for other opportunities to boost your revenue. Upsell attendees on coaching or additional courses. The real value often comes from the relationships built and the backend offers made, not just from ticket sales.

Why Hosting Smaller Events Can Be More Effective

Building a Core Community

One of the biggest advantages of hosting smaller events is the opportunity to build a loyal, engaged community. These aren't just attendees. They will return to future events, share their experience, and become your core audience. With a smaller event, it's not about selling out one big room. It's about creating lasting relationships.

Each event becomes a building block, and your audience grows with you over time. You're nurturing a group of repeat attendees rather than chasing the one-time crowd.

Managing Costs Wisely

Smaller events come with another major perk—lower costs. You have the flexibility to choose a venue that fits your budget, whether it's a modest meeting room or a cozy hotel space. With fewer attendees, food, AV, and other logistics become much more manageable. You won't be stuck trying to meet high minimums or locked into expensive vendor contracts. This keeps your stress levels in check and helps ensure your event is profitable, even on a smaller scale.

Deepening Engagement and Connection

There's something special about the intimacy of a small event. It's where the real magic happens. You're not just a speaker on stage; you're connecting with people face-to-face. Smaller settings naturally foster deeper engagement. Attendees feel seen, heard, and valued. This creates a sense of trust, and when people trust you, they're more likely to take action on your next offer. Whether it's joining your coaching program or signing up for a membership, their investment in you grows.

Maximizing Upsell Opportunities

Small events are also prime for upselling. When people spend a few days with you in person, they get to know you on a deeper level. By the time your event ends, you've built the trust and connection needed to confidently offer them the next step. Attendees are more likely to say yes to a coaching program, a membership, or a boot camp if they've had a personal, hands-on experience with you.

Learning and Scaling with Confidence

Starting small isn't just smart—it's sustainable. Smaller events allow you to learn the ropes without the high stakes of a large-scale production. As you gain confidence and learn what works, you can gradually increase the size of your events. You're managing profitability along the way, so when you do scale up, you're prepared and profitable from day one.

Quick Revenue Wins

Small events also give you immediate ways to generate revenue. Selling early bird tickets for next year's event while you're still at the current one is a great way to build momentum. Attendees are more likely to commit when they're still riding the high of the experience. On top of that, bring products like books, workbooks, or even T-shirts to sell at your event. These little extras can boost your income and create a more immersive experience for attendees.

Today's Exercise: Planning Your First In-Person Event

1. Define the Size and Scope

- Start by deciding how many people you want at your event. Keep it small—somewhere between 10 and 15 attendees is ideal for your first time.

- Get clear on the goal of the event. Are you looking to build a community? Or is the focus on generating revenue? Having a clear purpose will guide every decision moving forward.

2. Select a Simple Venue

- Look for cost-effective, intimate venues. Think local hotels, small meeting rooms, or even coworking spaces.

- Don't go overboard with venue size Remember, the more personal the setting, the more connected your attendees will feel. Aim for comfort and accessibility over flash.

3. Set Ticket Prices

- Your ticket price should reflect the value of a smaller, more personalized experience. Attendees are paying for access to you, so don't be afraid to charge a premium.

- Make sure your pricing also covers the basics—venue rental, food, and any other essential costs. Profit comes later; your first goal is to break even while delivering an unforgettable experience.

4. Create an Upsell Offer

- Plan ahead for how you'll offer something more at the event. Think of an additional coaching session or a boot camp that naturally flows from the content of the event.

- The upsell should be relevant to what they've just learned, offering a clear next step. It doesn't have to be complicated, just congruent with the event's theme.

5. Sell Early Bird Tickets for Your Next Event

- While your attendees are still in the room, offer them a special early bird discount for next year's event. This helps build momentum and gives you some upfront revenue for your next gathering.

○ Create urgency by making this a limited-time offer—give them a deadline to lock in their spot.

6. Capture Testimonials

○ Plan ahead to get video testimonials and photos during your event. This is your future marketing gold.

○ Set up a space at the event where attendees can comfortably share their thoughts. Make sure to ask open-ended questions that allow them to express how the event has impacted them. This will be invaluable for promoting future events.

By following these steps, you'll set yourself up for a successful and profitable first event. Keep it simple, stay focused, and let the experience teach you what to do next time.

Key Takeaways:

- Start small, stay focused: Smaller events build a core audience. They keep costs down and engage attendees more.

- Profit through upsells: The real profit of an event often comes from the upsell offers you present during or after it.

- Learn as you scale: Start small. It lets you master event hosting with low risk. It will build your confidence to grow over time.

19

The Coach's Mini Offer: 4-Week Group Coaching

In 1948, a handful of people gathered in a room to learn how to become better public speakers. They didn't know it, but they were part of something that would eventually become legendary. The course wasn't polished. It wasn't even fully planned. Dale Carnegie, the man leading the group, didn't have a step-by-step curriculum set in stone. Instead, he worked with his students. He listened to their struggles and breakthroughs.

Each session, Carnegie adjusted what he taught based on the feedback from his audience. He didn't waste time creating a perfect course upfront. Instead, he let the group's experiences guide him. This wasn't a mistake—it was the secret sauce that turned his approach into one of the most successful public speaking programs ever created.[7]

You can do the same with your group coaching offer. This chapter is about taking that leap before everything is built. You don't need a fully developed program to sell a coaching experience that delivers. You just need a clear vision of the transformation you want to offer and a willingness to adapt as you go.

Let's dive into how to use this strategy. It can help you create a successful coaching program. It should meet your audience's needs and be worth their money. Do this before you create any lessons.

Building in the Dark

Many coaches make the same mistake. They spend months crafting a full program, obsessing over every little detail. They create lesson plans, design slides, and refine their content, all without ever talking to their potential clients. Everything happens in a bubble based on assumptions.

Then comes launch day. They put their offer out into the world, expecting interest to pour in. Instead, they get silence. No sign-ups, no buzz. Just disappointment. Why? Because they've built something that doesn't actually serve the needs of their market.

The Assumption Trap

Relying on assumptions is a risky game. You think you know what your audience wants, but you haven't asked them. You haven't tested the waters. And when you don't get real feedback along the way, you're essentially guessing.

Without input from your ideal clients, it's like you're trying to solve a puzzle without seeing the full picture. Your program might sound great in your head, but if it doesn't solve a real, pressing problem for your audience, it's doomed to fall flat.

The Feedback-First Formula

There's a much smarter way to do this. Instead of spending months building something that might not sell, start by pre-selling a beta version of your 4-week group coaching program. Get real clients on board before you even begin creating the content. Let their feedback shape your program.

This approach does two things. It proves there's demand for your offer. It ensures you create a program that meets your audience's needs. Plus, you're getting paid to build it, instead of sinking time and money into something that might not work.

Find Out If They'll Pay

Pre-selling your group coaching lets you test the waters before you dive in. It's a reality check. If people aren't willing to pay for the transformation you're offering, you'll know before you've wasted time creating the whole thing. And that's valuable. You can tweak your messaging, pivot your focus, or even scrap the idea entirely if the demand just isn't there. Better to find that out now than after months of hard work.

Shape It to Their Needs

When you're working with a small beta group, their feedback is everything. You'll see, in real time, what resonates and what falls flat. That insight is priceless. You'll learn what your participants are truly struggling with, and you'll be able to shape your content to fit their exact needs. Instead of guessing what they need, you'll know. And that makes all the difference in delivering a coaching experience that hits the mark.

Get Paid While You Build

Most people build first and hope the money comes later. You're going to flip that script. By pre-selling, you're getting paid to create. Your beta clients are funding your program's development. So, you aren't investing time and money upfront. You're getting compensated for the value you're delivering as you fine-tune the content. It's a win-win.

Build Urgency

When something is limited, people move faster. By capping the number of participants and offering a special beta price, you create scarcity. People don't want to miss out. That urgency can drive sales in a way that a wide-open offer can't. When spots are limited, people feel the pressure to act before it's too late.

Flex as You Go

Every group is different. That's why flexibility is key. As you deliver your coaching sessions, you'll need to adapt based on the questions and feedback you get. Being willing to adjust on the fly means you're able to meet your group exactly where they are. It's not about sticking rigidly to a plan; it's about delivering what matters most in the moment.

Leverage Testimonials

Your beta participants are more than just clients—they're your first success stories. Their feedback and testimonials are pure gold when it comes to selling your final program. Nothing sells a program better than seeing real results from real people. When you take your coaching to a wider audience, these testimonials will provide the social proof you need to build trust and drive sales.

Today's Exercise: Build Your Group Coaching Offer in 30 Minutes

This exercise will walk you through creating your group coaching offer in just half an hour. You don't need to have everything figured out; just follow these steps, and you'll have a strong foundation to get started.

Define the Transformation

Start by writing down a clear, specific transformation your audience will experience in four weeks. Keep it simple. What will they walk away with by the end of your coaching program? It should be something measurable and achievable. For example, "By the end of this program, participants will have launched their first mini-course" or "Participants will have created a 30-day content plan for their blog." The more tangible the result, the better.

Outline Your 4-Week Curriculum

Now that you've defined the transformation, map out the key steps to get there. What major milestones do participants need to hit each week to achieve the final result? You don't need all the details yet—just think in broad strokes. For example:

- **Week 1:** Define the project and set clear goals

- **Week 2:** Plan and organize content

- **Week 3:** Create and refine the product

- **Week 4:** Launch and implement

These are just placeholders. The idea is to give yourself a rough roadmap that you'll develop as you go.

Set a Beta Price and Limit Enrollment

Decide on a price that feels like an easy "yes" for your audience. The beta version should be cheaper than the final product. But, it should cost enough for participants to feel invested. A sweet spot is often between $100 and $500, depending on the value you're offering. Also, limit enrollment to create exclusivity. Capping the group at 10 to 15 participants makes the offer feel special and encourages people to act fast.

Write a Simple Pitch

Next, craft a short email or social media post to announce your beta program. Keep it clear and to the point:

- Start with the transformation: What will participants achieve in four weeks?

- Emphasize the limited spots and the special beta pricing.

- Mention that they'll have a hand in shaping the final version of the program, which gives them added value.

Your goal here is to make the offer sound irresistible—something they can't afford to miss.

Launch to a Small, Warm Audience

Send your offer to a group of warm leads. These are people who already know you or have shown interest in your work. This could be a segment of your email list, social media followers, or previous clients. Pay close attention to their reactions and feedback. If you get positive responses and sign-ups, great! If not, use the feedback to adjust your offer before you open it up to a larger audience.

In just 30 minutes, you've laid the groundwork for your group coaching program. You don't need all the details yet; just enough to get it out there and start testing the waters.

Key Takeaways:

- **Pre-selling validates demand and reduces risk.** Selling your coaching program before creating it ensures there's a real need for your offer.

- **Tailoring your content based on feedback increases relevance and value.** Your beta participants' input helps you build a program that meets their exact needs.

- **Pre-sell group coaching to get paid while creating.** You don't have to invest time and energy upfront; your beta participants fund the program's development as you go.

20

The Coach's Main Offer: 1-on-1 Coaching

I remember thinking, "I wish I could get paid for my advice." I was working as an executive recruiter back then, spending hours on the phone every day. I'd help accounting professionals with job search tips, interview advice, and resume tweaks—all for free. The companies paid me for finding them the perfect employee. But, I felt I was giving away my valuable knowledge to the job applicants for nothing. Seven years of experience, countless tips, and strategies, all just handed out without a second thought.

One day, on a whim, I decided to see if anyone would actually pay for my advice. I slapped two PayPal buttons on a "Work With Me" page on my career coaching blog. The offers were simple: $50 for an hour of my time and $25 for 30 minutes. Looking back, I can see how underpriced I was—it's a mistake most of us make, undervaluing the knowledge we've spent years gathering. But still, for the next several months, I'd get three to five orders a week. It wasn't much, but I'd think to myself, "I can't make $50 an hour delivering pizzas." At the time, I couldn't think of another side job that would pay me $50 an hour.

That was the beginning. From those PayPal buttons to today, I've built coaching packages that have supported my clients and transformed their lives. But the biggest transformation? It was realizing the value of what I already knew—and how others would pay for it.

In this chapter, I want to show you how to start getting paid for your own advice.

Why Most Coaches Struggle to Get Paid

A lot of new coaches make the same mistake: they give away their best advice for free or charge way too little for their time. It's not because they don't know what they're doing. It's because they're unsure how to actually make money from what they know. They're waiting for some perfect moment—the day they feel "ready" or fully qualified. It's like they think they need to earn permission to charge what they're worth.

But that day never comes. You'll always feel like there's something else to learn, another certification to get, another experience to check off the list. So you keep holding back. Meanwhile, you're giving out golden nuggets of wisdom for free, hoping it'll somehow turn into paying clients down the road.

The Real Problem with This Approach

Here's the truth: underpricing yourself or handing out free advice doesn't work. People don't value what they get for free. If you give away too much without asking for anything in return, you send a message, whether you mean to or not. It suggests your expertise isn't worth paying for. And once people see you as "the free advice guy/gal," it's hard to change that perception.

Waiting for perfection is another trap. While you're waiting to feel "ready," opportunities are slipping by. Every day you hesitate is a day you could've been helping someone. You don't need to know everything to start making an impact. People pay you for your perspective, guidance, and experience. Not for some "perfect coach" version of you.

And if you're offering your advice for free, you're not creating any commitment on the client's end. When people don't pay, they don't take it seriously. They're not invested. A client who pays is a client who's ready to commit, take action, and get results.

How to Change Your Mindset and Approach

So what's the fix? Start now. Right where you are, with the knowledge you already have. You don't need to be the best in the world at what you do. You just need to be clear about the value you bring and how you can help someone get from where they are to where they want to be.

People aren't paying for your time—they're paying for the transformation you help them achieve. Focus on delivering results, not just showing up for an hour. When clients see that working with you will change their lives in some way, they'll gladly pay for that.

Finally, coaching should be treated like a real business, not a hobby. That means making your services easy to understand, your prices clear, and your offers accessible. People need to know exactly what they're getting when they decide to work with you. Don't make it complicated. The clearer you are, the more likely they are to say yes.

Why Clarity Is Everything

People don't take action when they're confused. If your coaching offers aren't crystal clear, potential clients will hesitate, unsure of what you're offering or how it benefits them. When you provide a simple, straightforward way to work with you, you remove that hesitation. Clients need to know exactly what they're getting—how much it costs, what's included, and what they can expect. Clarity removes friction, and with that friction gone, people are much more likely to commit.

Small Wins Build Confidence

You don't have to jump into high-ticket offers right away. In fact, starting small might be the best way to build your confidence as a coach. Create simple, affordable coaching packages that are easy for people to say yes to. These smaller offers not only allow you to gain experience but also help you refine your process and get better at delivering results. Each small win, both for you and your clients, adds up and builds your confidence for bigger offers down the road.

Payment Equals Commitment

When people pay, they pay attention. Financial investment creates a sense of commitment. When clients invest their hard-earned money, they're more likely to show up, do the work, and take your coaching seriously. It's not just about the money—it's about creating a sense of value for both you and the client. Pricing yourself right tells the client, "This is worth it." If they see your coaching as valuable, they'll commit more to the process.

Niche Down to Attract the Right Clients

Not everyone is your ideal client. The more specific you are about who you help and how you help them, the easier it becomes to attract the right people. When you narrow down your niche, you're able to deliver higher-quality, more personalized coaching. Clients who see themselves in your messaging will be much more willing to pay for your services. They know you're the right fit for their unique challenges, and that's what makes your coaching valuable to them.

Clear Communication Builds Trust

People need to know exactly how your coaching can benefit them. If you leave things vague or ambiguous, they're less likely to trust that you can help. Be clear about the outcomes you provide and how you'll get them there. When clients can see a clear path to their goals, they'll feel more confident in hiring you. And trust isn't just built through your results—it's built through how you communicate those results before they even start working with you.

Today's Exercise: Create Your First Coaching Offer

Let's get hands-on. This exercise will guide you through creating your first coaching offer. Follow these simple steps to get started:

Step 1: Decide on Your Coaching Niche. Who can you help most effectively? Think about your experience, knowledge, and skills. Who do you feel confident guiding? Is it aspiring entrepreneurs? Are people navigating career changes? Health and fitness enthusiasts? The more specific, the better. Pick a niche that matches your strengths.

Step 2: Set a Simple Price. Don't get stuck overthinking pricing. Just pick a number that feels fair for the value you're offering. You could start with an hourly rate (say, $50 per hour) or a package deal (like four sessions for $200). The key is to get something down so you can start. Remember, you can always adjust your pricing as you gain more experience and confidence.

Step 3: Define 3 Outcomes You Can Deliver. Clients pay for results. What specific outcomes can you help people achieve? Write down three clear, measurable results they'll get from working with you. Examples might be: "Help you lose 10 pounds in 6 weeks," or "Guide you through creating a 30-day career transition plan." Be as specific as possible—vague promises won't sell. Clients want to know what success looks like when they hire you.

Step 4: Build Your 'Work With Me' Page. Now, it's time to put it all together. On your website, create a dedicated "Work With Me" page. Write a short description of your coaching offer, highlight the three outcomes you've defined, and clearly list your pricing. Make it easy for people to take action—include a simple way to book a session or schedule a call. You can use tools like Calendly or a basic email link.

Step 5: Share and Promote. Once your "Work With Me" page is live, share it! Post it on your blog, website, or social media channels. You could even mention it in your email newsletter if you have one. The goal is to let people know that you're officially offering coaching services and are ready to help. Invite them to book a session and take the first step toward achieving their goals.

By the end of this exercise, you'll have a clear coaching offer that's out in the world, giving potential clients a straightforward way to work with you. Start small, and don't worry about making it perfect. The important thing is that you've taken action.

Key Takeaways:

- You don't need to be perfect to start coaching—begin with what you know, and clients will pay for the value you bring.

- Clear communication and specific outcomes are key to attracting the right clients and getting them to commit.

- Treat your coaching like a business by setting clear prices, defining results, and creating an easy way for clients to book your services.

21

The Coach's Max Offer: A Coaching Membership

I n 2017, I hit a wall. My coaching business was growing, but my time wasn't. Sure, I loved the one-on-one work with clients. It's rewarding to help someone break through in real-time. But there was only one of me, and no matter how much I charged or how efficient I became, there were only so many hours in a day. It wasn't sustainable.

That's when I realized something had to change. I wasn't going to stop coaching, but I had to find a way to scale it. The question was: how do you grow something so personal without losing its magic?

So, I decided to experiment. I launched what I now call a "coaching membership." To my surprise, it sold out in just three hours. I began testing my idea with a small beta group of clients. What started as a tiny test grew into a $5,000-a-month revenue stream in 90 days. And the best part? It only took 3-5 hours per week to run it.

This chapter is about how you can create the same thing. If you're feeling like I did, maxed out on hours, and wondering how to keep growing, you're in the right place. We're going to dive into what it takes to build a large-scale, group coaching membership—one that works year-round and doesn't leave you burnt out.

The best part? You don't need to sacrifice quality or personal connection to do it. Let's get into it.

Stuck in the Coaching Maze

Most coaches fall into the one-on-one coaching trap. They spend countless hours giving personalized advice to each client, and while it works, there's a hard limit on how far this can take you. Don't get me wrong. When you are first getting started, one-on-one coaching is a great way to get results and build your coaching skills. But there are only so many hours in a day, and eventually, the number of clients you can take on hits a ceiling. You can raise your rates, but that only buys you a bit more time before you're maxed out again.

The real issue isn't just time. It's energy. One-on-one coaching is draining, and as your client list grows, so do the demands on you. You're left juggling multiple people's needs, and it doesn't take long before you start feeling stretched too thin.

The Time Trap

Trading time for money might work for a while, but it's a ticking clock. The more clients you take on, the more hours you need to work. Your income can only grow as fast as your availability. It's a classic catch-22: you want to help more people, but you also want to live your life. And it's easy to get stuck thinking you can do both if you just try harder. But eventually, it catches up with you. Burnout sets in.

Burnout doesn't just affect your energy levels—it impacts the quality of your coaching. You stop showing up fully present for your clients, and that's when things start to break down. It's frustrating because deep down, you know there's more potential. You just can't get there without sacrificing something important.

Scaling with a Coaching Membership

What if you didn't have to choose between helping more people and keeping your sanity? This is where shifting to a group coaching model comes in. Instead of trying to manage dozens of one-on-one clients, you can move to a system that scales—without adding more hours to your schedule.

A coaching membership allows you to reach more clients, offer more value, and still show up fully. Imagine being able to coach 60 people in a week, all while working fewer hours than you would with ten one-on-one clients. It's about scaling your impact, not your time. And the best part? You still get to keep the personal touch that makes coaching so powerful.

The Coaching Membership: Personalized Coaching Without the Grind

Imagine coaching many clients without working more hours or feeling drained. A coaching membership makes this possible. It's not just a system—it's a game changer. You get to maintain the personal connection that makes coaching so powerful, but with a structure that scales. No more back-to-back one-on-one sessions that leave you exhausted. Instead, you provide value to a group while still offering personalized support that makes clients feel seen and heard.

In this model, your role shifts from being a full-time coach to a leader and guide. Your members receive coaching, resources, and a sense of community—all without adding to your workload. How? It all comes down to three core pillars: Coaching, Courses, and Community. Let's break them down.

Pillar 1. Coaching: Personalized Guidance at Scale

The heart of any coaching membership is the coaching itself. But it differs from traditional one-on-one coaching. You won't sit on endless calls, repeating the same advice to different people. Instead, you create an environment where group coaching feels just as personal as individual sessions.

How do you do this? By using co-working and laser coaching sessions. Here is how it works: your members join a weekly call where they have two options. They can either participate in a focused co-working session or raise their hand for laser coaching. Co-working sessions let your clients get things done in a supportive, accountability-driven environment. They're all working on their individual projects, but there's a shared energy that keeps everyone focused.

Then, those who need more can opt for laser coaching—quick, targeted one-on-one feedback in a breakout room. It's just 10 minutes, but it's enough to address specific challenges and provide clarity. You help them solve real problems without the long, drawn-out sessions. The best part? You're not burning out. In just a few hours each week, you're providing high-value coaching to a large group of people, all while keeping your energy intact. It's a smarter way to coach, and your members feel like they're getting your full attention.

Pillar 2. Courses: Evergreen Resources that Grow with Your Membership

Coaching is powerful, but you don't want to spend all your time explaining the same concepts over and over. That's where your course library comes in. With a coaching membership, your courses become an essential part of the value you offer. Members don't just come for the live coaching—they also get access to a vault of resources that they can use whenever they need.

This isn't just a random collection of videos. It's a carefully curated library designed to support your clients on their journey. Whether they need help with specific strategies, mindset shifts, or practical steps, there's a course for that. And here's the best part: it's always growing. As you create new courses, they automatically get added to the membership. You're building a treasure chest of content that continues to deliver value, month after month, without any extra effort on your part.

Think of it as giving your members a roadmap. They can dive into these courses at any time, working at their own pace, and come to coaching calls with targeted questions. This frees you up from repeating yourself while your members get the exact resources they need, exactly when they need them. It's a win-win.

Pillar 3. Community: The Glue That Keeps Members Engaged

There's something about being part of a group with a shared mission. It motivates people in ways that nothing else can. Your coaching membership isn't just about coaching or courses—it's about creating a community where success thrives. When people feel connected to others who share their goals, they're more likely to stay engaged and take action.

This sense of belonging is the third pillar of a coaching membership. It's what keeps people coming back after the initial excitement fades. You build community by fostering regular interaction. Use weekly Zoom calls, discussion threads, group challenges, and live events. These aren't just check-ins. They're opportunities for members to learn from each other, celebrate wins, and support each other through setbacks.

And it doesn't stop at virtual events. Consider hosting exclusive boot camps or even an annual live event where members get together in person. They strengthen community bonds. They create experiences that go beyond learning—they build relationships. When your members feel like they're part of something bigger, they're not just joining a program. They're joining a movement. That's the glue that holds your membership together.

A coaching membership, based on these three pillars—Coaching, Courses, and Community—creates a structure. It lets you serve more clients while protecting your time and energy. It's a model that scales without sacrificing the personal touch that makes coaching so impactful. Each pillar is vital. Together, they form a sustainable, thriving membership. It keeps members engaged and coming back year after year.

Today's Exercise: Drafting Your Coaching Membership Plan

In this exercise, you'll draft a plan. It will map out how to implement the three key pillars of your coaching membership: Coaching, Courses, and Community. By the end, you'll have a clear vision of how to structure your membership to provide value at scale while protecting your time.

1. Define Your Coaching Structure

First, consider how to run your coaching sessions. You must balance personal support with group dynamics. Use the following questions to guide your draft:

- How often will you host live coaching sessions? Weekly, bi-weekly, or monthly?

- Will you offer a mix of co-working sessions and laser coaching? If so, what will that look like?

- How long will each coaching session last, and how many people can participate at once?

- For laser coaching, how will you handle private sessions in a group setting (e.g., breakout rooms)?

- What tools will you use (Zoom, Slack, or another platform) to facilitate your coaching sessions?

Write It Out: Draft a schedule for your coaching sessions. Outline how each session will run, including the mix between co-working and coaching. Make it clear how you will manage your time and give your members the personalized attention they need.

Example: *I will host a 90-minute live session every Monday at 12 PM. The main Zoom room will be a co-working session. The rest will be 10-minute laser coaching slots. I'll use Zoom breakout rooms for private one-on-one sessions.*

2. Build Your Course Library

Now, focus on the resources your members will have access to. Start by thinking about the core topics you want to cover and how your course library will grow over time.

- What existing courses or training can you include in your membership right now?

- What new content could you create to support your members' needs?

- How often will you add new content or update your course library?

- Will your courses be step-by-step or more flexible, allowing members to pick what they need at any time?

Write It Out: Create a list of the courses and resources that will be available when someone joins your membership. Map out a plan for how you will continue adding content over time.

Example: *My membership will launch with five core courses: 1) Building Your Online Platform, 2) Content Creation Made Simple, 3) Scaling Your Coaching Business, 4) Email Marketing Strategies, and 5) Growing Your Community. I will add a new course every quarter based on member feedback and needs.*

3. Cultivate Your Community

The third pillar is creating a sense of belonging that keeps members engaged. This requires regular interaction and opportunities for your members to connect, not just with you, but with each other.

- What types of community events will you offer (e.g., group Zoom calls, challenges, live events)?

- How will members interact between calls (e.g., through a Slack group, Facebook group, or another platform)?

- How will you encourage members to engage with each other and share their progress?

Write It Out: Draft a plan for how you'll foster community within your membership. Include specific ideas for events and engagement activities to keep your members active and connected.

Example: *I will host a live group call every Wednesday for members to share their wins, ask questions, and support each other. We'll also do quarterly challenges where members work on specific goals together, with prizes for those who reach their targets. Between sessions, members will use a private Slack group. I'll be there to answer questions and give feedback.*

4. Putting It All Together

Once you've drafted your ideas for each pillar, take a step back and look at the bigger picture. How do these three pillars fit together? Are there any adjustments you need to make to balance coaching, content, and community?

Finally, refine your plan by asking yourself:

- How can I make the coaching sessions more efficient while still providing value?

- Does my course library offer the right resources at the right time?

- What can I do to make my community feel more engaged and connected?

This draft is the foundation of your coaching membership. With these three pillars in place, you'll have a model that scales your impact while giving your members everything they need to succeed.

Key Takeaways:

- A coaching membership lets you serve more clients at scale. You can use co-working sessions, laser coaching, and evergreen resources. It reduces your time commitment.

- A growing course library adds great value to your members. It requires little effort, and it gives them access to tools they can use anytime.

- A strong sense of community keeps members engaged and loyal. It creates a support system where shared goals and relationships drive success.

22

The 48-Day Blueprint to Scale Your Income

Congratulations! You've made it through the journey of scaling your income, and that's no small achievement. You've taken the time to learn and reflect, and now you stand ready to implement strategies that can truly transform your business. This is a moment to feel proud. Not everyone will take that first step. Fewer still will endure the uncertainties of growing an audience and creating multiple income streams.

As you move forward, it's normal to feel a bit unsure at times. Implementation can bring hurdles and challenges. But, your insights and perspective matter. The world needs your message, and only you can deliver it in a way that resonates with the people you are meant to serve. Never underestimate the power of your voice, even if your audience starts small. Many successful creators began with just a handful of followers, but they stayed true to their passion, and that's what made all the difference.

The strategies in this book have equipped you with the tools you need to overcome the most common hurdles in audience building. Whether it's creating a low-content book, launching a virtual workshop, or designing your first mini-course, you now have a clear path to follow. But the real key is to create content from the heart. It's not about the size of your audience; it's about showing up consistently, providing value, and letting your message resonate with those who need it.

Stay optimistic and continue to take action. Your dream of making an impact and earning an income from your message is not only possible—it's within reach. Every successful creator once stood where you are now, and the ones who made it were the ones who kept going. Your journey is just beginning, and I'm excited to see the impact you'll make.

If you're looking for additional support, don't forget about the companion workbook to this book. It's designed to reinforce key concepts and help you stay motivated as you continue to grow your audience and scale your income. You've got this!

Your voice is needed, and the world is waiting to hear your message. Keep moving forward—you're closer to your goals than you realize.

The 48-Day Blueprint to Scale Your Income

Welcome to the **48-Day Blueprint** section, designed to help you implement and launch any of the 12 income streams outlined in this book. Each blueprint outlines a 48-day process in manageable steps. It keeps you focused and prevents overwhelm.

Here's how it works:

- Each income stream starts with **6 Days of Planning** to lay a solid foundation before you begin.

- The next **five weeks are divided into weekly sprint goals**; each focused on making progress toward your launch.

- Have a draft product ready to go in **under 48 days!**

These blueprints will give you a clear roadmap. It will help you create and launch new offers. They could be a low-content book, a paid workshop, or a coaching program. Choose the income stream that resonates most with you, stick to the timeline, and watch your income grow!

Low-Content Book (Writer Mini Offer)

- **6-Days of Planning:** Research your niche and outline a low-content book (journal, planner, or workbook) based on your audience's needs.

- **Week 1:** Draft 10-15 templates or pages for the book.

- **Week 2:** Complete the remaining content for the book and format it.

- **Week 3:** Design the cover and layout using tools like Canva or hire a designer.

- **Week 4:** Upload the book to self-publishing platforms (Amazon KDP, Etsy, etc.).

- **Week 5:** Create a simple landing page to promote your book and launch it to your email list and social media.

Compact Book (Writer Main Offer)

- **6-Days of Planning:** Outline the book's core message and structure (10-12 chapters).

- **Week 1:** Write the first two chapters (5,000 words total).

- **Week 2:** Write two more chapters, focusing on adding value and actionable steps.

- **Week 3:** Complete the first draft of the remaining chapters.

- **Week 4:** Edit, format, and design the cover.

- **Week 5:** Publish on Amazon, set up pre-launch emails, and promote the launch.

Book Series (Writer Max Offer)

- **6-Days of Planning:** Plan the series' overall theme and outline each book's main topics.

- **Week 1:** Write the first 2-3 chapters of the first book.

- **Week 2:** Continue writing, focusing on completing the first draft of the first book.

- **Week 3:** Finalize edits, design the book cover, and format for print and digital.

- **Week 4:** Publish the first book and begin writing the second book in the series.

- **Week 5:** Develop a launch strategy for the entire series, building excitement for future releases.

Mini-Course (Teacher Mini Offer)

- **6-Days of Planning:** Outline the mini-course, breaking it into 7-10 lessons.

- **Week 1:** Record two video lessons.

- **Week 2:** Record the remaining lessons and draft any worksheets or resources.

- **Week 3:** Edit videos and create an accompanying workbook or handout.

- **Week 4:** Upload the course to your platform (Teachable, Kajabi, etc.) and set up sales pages.

- **Week 5:** Launch to your email list and promote on social media with a limited-time offer.

Flagship Course (Teacher Main Offer)

- **6-Days of Planning:** Develop the course outline (3-7 modules) and create a detailed lesson plan.

- **Week 1:** Record the first two modules.

- **Week 2:** Record the next two modules and gather/create worksheets, slides, and additional content.

- **Week 3:** Finalize recording and begin editing the entire course.

- **Week 4:** Set up the course on your platform and build the sales funnel.

- **Week 5:** Launch a webinar or live event to promote the course to your audience.

Membership Site (Teacher Max Offer)

- **6-Days of Planning:** Define the core value of your membership and decide on a content delivery schedule (monthly, weekly).

- **Week 1:** Create the first two months of content and build out the member portal.

- **Week 2:** Develop the member community space (Facebook Group, private forum).

- **Week 3:** Record your welcome video, create onboarding materials, and finalize membership pricing.

- **Week 4:** Set up the membership sales funnel and prepare a launch campaign.

- **Week 5:** Launch to your email list with early bird pricing and bonuses to drive sign-ups.

Paid Virtual Workshop (Speaker Mini Offer)

- **6-Days of Planning:** Choose a topic and create a 60-90 minute outline for the virtual workshop.

- **Week 1:** Create slides and script for the workshop.

- **Week 2:** Record a short promotional video and start advertising the workshop.

- **Week 3:** Host the workshop live, recording it for future use.

- **Week 4:** Edit the workshop recording and package it for evergreen sales.

- **Week 5:** Create a follow-up sequence for attendees and promote the recorded version.

Paid Speaking Gigs (Speaker Main Offer)

- **6-Days of Planning:** Identify key topics and create a pitch for potential speaking gigs.

- **Week 1:** Create a speaker demo reel and update your speaking page.

- **Week 2:** Reach out to event organizers and pitch your talk.

- **Week 3:** Continue pitching and set up follow-up systems to secure bookings.

- **Week 4:** Deliver your first talk and gather testimonials or feedback.

- **Week 5:** Follow up with contacts, refine your pitch, and schedule future gigs.

Host In-Person Events (Speaker Max Offer)

- **6-Days of Planning:** Decide on the event theme and structure (1-day, 2-day workshop).

- **Week 1:** Secure a venue and outline your event schedule.

- **Week 2:** Promote the event to your audience and offer early bird pricing.

- **Week 3:** Finalize speakers, sponsors, and vendors if necessary.

- **Week 4:** Organize logistics, including audio/visual needs, catering, and materials.

- **Week 5:** Host the event and gather testimonials or feedback for future marketing.

4-Week Group Coaching Program (Coach Mini Offer)

- **6-Days of Planning:** Choose the topic and create the structure for a 4-week program (weekly coaching calls).

- **Week 1:** Write outlines for each week's coaching session and gather resources for your clients.

- **Week 2:** Promote the program to your list, focusing on scarcity and limited spots.

- **Week 3:** Begin the first group session and gather feedback from participants.

- **Week 4:** Create a next-step offer with ongoing support options (upsell).

- **Week 5:** Package the recorded sessions into a digital product or evergreen offer.

1-on-1 Coaching (Coach Main Offer)

- **6-Days of Planning:** Define your coaching package and decide on pricing and structure.

- **Week 1:** Set up a "Work with Me" page with clear details about your coaching program.

- **Week 2:** Promote to your email list and create a process for booking discovery calls.

- **Week 3:** Start offering free discovery calls to interested clients.

- **Week 4:** Onboard your first coaching clients and develop personalized plans for them.

- **Week 5:** Gather testimonials and create a system for client retention and referrals.

Coaching Membership (Coach Max Offer)

- **6-Days of Planning:** Define the value proposition and content delivery for your coaching membership.

- **Week 1:** Set up a membership platform and decide on the monthly content (e.g., group coaching calls and workshops).

- **Week 2:** Record your welcome video and create a member onboarding experience.

- **Week 3:** Start promoting the membership to your current clients and list.

- **Week 4:** Host your first group call or live event within the membership.

- **Week 5:** Gather feedback, refine content, and promote the next enrollment phase.

These blueprints will help you stay on track during the 48-day period. They will guide you in taking consistent action to launch each income stream.

23

What's Next?

Congratulations on completing *Scale Your Income*!

You've taken a huge step toward diversifying your revenue streams and scaling your business as a writer, coach, teacher, or speaker. By now, you've gained valuable insights into creating multiple income streams, and you're well on your way to achieving financial freedom.

But as you reflect on what you've accomplished, you might be asking yourself, "What's next?" Now that you've mastered the art of scaling your income, how can you build on that momentum to ensure long-term success?

The answer lies in something crucial to any thriving business: **email list monetization.**

Too many marketers burn out their email lists by constantly pushing direct sales. But what if there were a better way? What if you could guide your subscribers on a seamless journey, inviting them to the next step rather than pushing them to buy?

That's exactly what you'll discover in the next book of this series: *Monetize Your List.*

In Monetize Your List, I introduce the Diamond Customer Journey Map. It's a unique framework to help you nurture your subscribers, without aggressive selling.

This framework uses a fun, easy-to-understand baseball analogy to walk you through the customer journey:

- **1st base**: Leads (subscribers show interest by joining your list)

- **2nd base**: Clicks (subscribers click through to engage with your content)

- **3rd base**: Sales (subscribers make a purchase)

- **Home base**: Onboarding (new customers are welcomed and nurtured)

The Diamond Customer Journey Map keeps your audience engaged. It invites them to take the next step, like clicking a link or making a purchase. But, it avoids overwhelming them with constant sales pitches.

This approach builds trust and keeps your email list engaged, instead of burning them out.

By using this method, you'll turn subscribers into loyal customers without ever feeling like you're "selling." The key is to guide them, not push them. And in *Monetize Your List*, you'll get the full playbook on how to make it work for your business.

So, are you ready to continue your journey and discover how to maximize the potential of your email list?

Get ready to dive into *Monetize Your List* and transform your subscribers into raving fans who can't wait to work with you!

Grab your copy of "*Monetize Your List: The 90-Day Game Plan to Automate Sales with Your Email List as a Writer, Coach, Teacher or Speaker*" today at PlatformGrowthBooks.com.

Your financial freedom is waiting. Let's go monetize your list together!

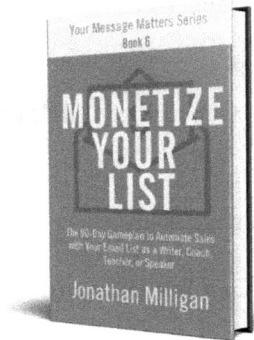

Thank You

I want to express my gratitude for choosing and purchasing my book. In a world overflowing with choices, you selected mine, and for that, I'm truly thankful.

Before we part ways, may I request a minor favor? Would it be too much to ask for you to leave a review on the platform? For an independent author like myself, receiving direct reader feedback through reviews significantly contributes to the success of the work.

Your insights will guide me in creating content that effectively aids you in achieving your desired results. Your feedback is highly valuable to me. Thank you for your time and consideration.

Leave a review by going to: **JMill.Biz/Scale-Review**

1. McGlade, Conor. "The Rise, Fall, and Potential Comeback of Toys 'R' Us." *Thomasnet*, 3 Mar. 2022, www.thomasnet.com. Accessed 28 Oct. 2024.

2. Silvestre, Dan. "Start With Why by Simon Sinek: Summary and Notes." *Dan Silvestre*, dansilvestre.com, Accessed 28 Oct. 2024.

3. Johnson, Nick. "The First Wendy's Menu Only Featured Five Savory Items." *The Daily Meal*, 22 Apr. 2023, www.thedailymeal.com.

4. Fluker, Elayne. "Fitlosophy CEO Angela Mader on Starting Small, Looking Big, Launching Your Products & Building a Great Brand." *Elayne Fluker*, elaynefluker.com. Accessed 28 Oct. 2024.

5. Doctorow, Cory. "How to Use Google AdWords to Prototype and Test a Book Title." *Boing Boing*, 25 Oct. 2010, boingboing.net.

6. "A Look at TED, from 1984 through the Present." *TED Blog*, blog.ted.com. Accessed 28 Oct. 2024.

7. "The Dale Carnegie Course in Effective Speaking, Human Relations, and Leadership." *Dale Carnegie & Associates, Inc.*, archive.org. Accessed 28 Oct. 2024.